METALLICA

UNCENSORED

ON THE RECORD

BY TOM KING

CODA
BOOKS LTD

C⊕DA
BOOKS LTD

www.codabooks.com

This edition is published in Great Britain in 2012 by

Coda Books Ltd., Office Suite 2, Shrieves Walk, 39 Sheep Street, Stratford-upon-Avon, Warwickshire CV37 6GJ

www.codbooks.com

Copyright © 2012 by Coda Books Ltd.

Photographs courtesy of Pictorial Press.

A CIP catalogue record for this book is available from the British Library.

ISBN: 978-1-78158-199-5

MUSIC REVIEWS LTD

CONTENTS

3

INTRODUCTION

BLACK SABBATH may have invented heavy metal, and bands such as Judas Priest, Iron Maiden, Motörhead, Slayer, Death and Venom may have pioneered its many subgenres, but Metallica are without a doubt the biggest and most successful metal band in existence. Currently the seventh-biggest recording act in American history, the American quartet have sold over 85 million records in various formats across their 25-year career and – at the time of writing – show little sign of slowing down, despite being in their forties.

Metallica's career falls into distinct stages, due to changes both in musical direction and fluctuations in their commercial fortunes, and so it's been convenient to divide this text into four chronological sections. Between their formation in 1981 and the tragic loss of their second, pioneering bass player Cliff Burton five years later, Metallica performed a brand of thrash metal, a subspecies of the heavy metal parent, which emerged jointly from San Francisco's Bay Area and Newcastle in 1981 and 1982. Honing the original sound into a melodic, almost progressive recipe that was all their own, the band toured incessantly, partied hard and were on the point of great things when Burton died.

The story then moves from 1987 through a pivotal change of style until 1995 – a much longer span of time justified by the fact that more or less all the band did from 1992 to 1995 was tour, albeit on a vast scale. 1991's self-titled 'Black Album' is the focal point of this chapter, Metallica's best-selling album to date and the one which catapulted them out of clubs into stadiums. Controversial and yet mainstream, this album's story could take up an entire book.

After this Metallica's fortunes took a downturn, as they experimented with an alternative rock approach that gained them few new fans and the disgust of most of their older fanbase. Touring revenue remained high, but the records of the era were never destined to be career high points. Worse was to come when drummer Lars Ulrich represented the band's lawsuit against the Napster file-sharing program, ultimately helping in its downfall.

Finally, I've brought the story up to date with a run-through of the tumultous, and some might say most important years of the band's career. After the Napster debacle, personnel shifts, public disputes and addiction problems, Metallica embarked on a two-year period in which they were trailed by a camera crew for a feature film, recorded another controversial album, St. Anger, and reassessed their priorities for the future.

It's quite a ride, and not easy to pack into a mere 20,000 words. You'll note that musical analysis is minimal – that has been reserved for the track-by-track rundown that accompanies the main text. Enjoy!

Tom King, 2006

THE STORY OF METALLICA

I N 1980, heavy metal was at a crossroads, with the pioneers of the genre struggling for critical air-time and fans looking for new sounds.

The original metal band, Black Sabbath, had seen its best-known vocalist – Ozzy Osbourne – depart two years before and had recruited Ronnie James Dio, the sometime singer of Rainbow, for vocals on their new album Heaven And Hell, a worthy effort but hardly of the calibre of their 70s material. Judas Priest were ploughing the same furrow they had begun in 1974 with their debut album, Rocka Rolla, with some success, but their studs-and-leather formula was starting to look a little hackneyed in the wake of the punk movement, which had reached its peak in 1978.

The year before, a new type of metal had begun to make its presence felt in the UK with a swathe of bands who had emerged from the underground clubs and pubs of the cities – primarily London, Newcastle and Birmingham. Dubbed by Sounds editor Alan Lewis and reporter Geoff Barton the New Wave Of British Heavy Metal (NWOBHM), the new groups played faster, harder and heavier than their predecessors and – despite being signed to small record labels with little budget, at least initially – slowly made an overseas impact.

The leaders of the NWOBHM had been established by 1981 as Def Leppard, Iron Maiden, Saxon, Angel Witch, Blitzkrieg and Diamond Head, with literally hundreds more in their wake. Of this list, Leppard and Maiden went on to carve out enormous careers by the middle of the decade, with legions of fans devoted to their harmonious but riff-heavy tunes and uncompromising image.

Among these bands was a Newcastle outfit called Venom, a trio comprising bassist/vocalist Conrad Lant, guitarist Jeff Dunn and drummer Tony Bray. Adopting the stage names of Cronos, Mantas and Abaddon – a then-new tactic of using demonic motifs to scare the establishment and attract followers – the band played poorly but with commitment, issuing a debut album in January 1981 entitled Welcome To Hell. Full of Satanic themes and much faster than anything metal fans had heard before, the LP became recognised as the first thrash metal album and caused enormous ripples in the heavy metal community, even though its creators never gained the commercial rewards they deserved.

One young headbanger who was impressed by the Venom approach was the 17-year-old Lars Ulrich, a Californian resident who had moved to the US from his home country of Denmark in the late 1970s to pursue his two main interests – rock music and tennis. His father, Torben Ulrich, was a cultured, educated sportsman who had risen to the status of Denmark's top tennis player in the previous decade and also followed a parallel career as a music journalist, musician and artist. Jazz was his field, and he was connected to the American scene already: Lars' godfather was the renowned Dexter Gordon, although the two didn't know each other well.

Why did the family make the move? "I think it was a complex of things," said Torben later. "In those years I was beginning to go back and forth and play tennis out of Denmark. I was writing about music for the Danish newspapers, and travelling to London and New York to write, or maybe also to play tennis. All those years we were operating in and out of Denmark. Lars' grandparents had a large house on the coastline west of [the Danish town of] Elsinore, so we could be there a lot and we could also be in town where we had this house. And then Lars went to school there and I would come back there."

"But then in the late 70s things changed," Torben continued. "Lars' mother's parents died and I had begun to play more and more in the Grand Masters, a tour for the older players. There were more and more tournaments in Hong Kong and so on, and I felt that it was harder and harder for me to get back to Denmark from these places. And also, as you get older it becomes more stressful to travel so extensively. I felt that I needed more rest in between… So we thought if we moved [to the US] for a little while that all these things would be addressed, and Lars could see which way he wanted to go."

The Ulrich family was well-connected: "Before Lars was born I played music and visited London," recalled Torben. "I was friends with Chris Barber, who is a trombonist who plays traditional jazz music. Humphrey Lyttelton, too. I would play with him at 100 Oxford Street, we'd spend a lot of time there… I was a student of Sidney Bechet's work, both before I knew him and later on. Even in the late 40s I was interested in him. I travelled to France and saw some bands who were playing in the style of King Oliver and Louis Armstrong: Bechet was a big hero there, and I tried to get to Paris as often as I could to be around him."

Torben and his wife Lone took Lars to settle in a wealthy town house in Los Angeles where they knew the school and sports facilities were good: the Ulrichs also knew a few people in the neighbourhood and the young man settled in rapidly. Although he embraced the local rock scene wholeheartedly – an early memory for him was attending a concert in LA by his lifelong idols, Deep Purple – he also remained in touch with the European scene through subscriptions to UK magazines such as Sounds. A huge fan of the NWOBHM, Lars had ambitions by the time he was 13 of starting a band, and had in fact been given a drum kit by his grandmother by the time he had entered his mid-teens. Although he didn't master the kit until at least

1981, this didn't deter him from placing an ad in the famed LA newspaper Recycler, which included a Musicians Wanted section browsed by all the city's wannabe rock stars.

One musician who answered Lars' ad was James Alan Hetfield, an introverted but likeable guitarist who was a fan of stadium-rockers such as Aerosmith and Ted Nugent. Hetfield, who lived in a household dominated by the Christian Scientist beliefs of his parents, had little time for the undeveloped drum skills of Ulrich, and their first meeting came to nothing. Nonetheless, the two noted each other's interest in rock music and would meet again before long.

James later told Playboy: "I was raised as a Christian Scientist, which is a strange religion. The main rule is, God will fix everything. Your body is just a shell, you don't need doctors. It was alienating and hard to understand. I couldn't get a physical to play football. It was weird having to leave health class during school, and all the kids saying, 'Why do you have to leave? Are you some kind of freak?' As a kid, you want to be part of the team. They're always whispering about you and thinking you're weird. That was very upsetting. My dad taught Sunday school – he was into it. It was pretty much forced upon me. We had these little testimonials, and there was a girl that had her arm broken. She stood up and said, 'I broke my arm but now, look, it's all better'. But it was just, like, mangled. Now that I think about it, it was pretty disturbing".

Musically, James was a committed rock fan. As he told Rolling Stone: "Probably the most memorable [show I remember] was the California World Music Festival. It was one of those two-day things. The first night was Ted Nugent and Van Halen – no, Aerosmith. I must have been 15 or 16. I remember following around my buddy, who was selling drugs. He tore up a part of his ticket – it had a kind of rainbow edge – and he cut it into bits and sold it as acid. I was like, what are you doing, man? He used the money to buy beer. I was a huge Aerosmith fan. I couldn't believe I was seeing them so close. I worked my way up there as far as I could. There was something magical about seeing them as actual live people, not just pictures on an album. The real coolness of Joe Perry, especially. It's impossible for him to be uncool. And I remember I was blown away by the fact that Steven was calling the crowd 'motherfuckers'. I was like, whoa – are you supposed to do that?"

In the summer of 1981, Lars took a trip to the UK to meet the band he worshipped most on the NWOBHM circuit – Diamond Head. Arriving at a show with very little money, he approached and befriended the band and spent much time with them, eventually sleeping on the bandmembers' floors for three months and learning much about the life of a rock band. After returning to the US, he stayed in touch with them by letter, often stating that he intended to start a band of his own and wondering why Diamond Head had not yet taken the rock scene by storm. Their guitarist Brian Tatler recalled: "He was saying, by the way, I've formed a band called Metallica and we're rehearsing

six hours a day, six days a week – or something like that – and we've got this guitarist who's pretty good, he's pretty fast. And I thought wow, they're really going for it."

This time Lars made serious efforts to hone a drum technique, spurred into action by the friends he had made on the LA metal scene – one of whom was Brian Slagel, a record store worker who published a fanzine and had ambitions towards starting a record label. In due course Slagel decided to compile an LP of the local metal bands that had sprung up in the wake of inspirational musical movements such as the NWOBHM, and used the contacts in record distribution from his store to set up distribution for it. He mentioned in passing to Lars that a space had become available on the record – which he intended to call Metal Massacre – and Ulrich immediately asked if he could record a song for it, undeterred by the fact that he had no band, no song, hardly any recording equipment and only the most basic drumming skills.

Calling up Hetfield, with whom he had endured such an unpromising rehearsal the previous year, Lars arranged an impromptu songwriting session and a track was actually created, titled 'Hit The Lights' and featuring a solo from a local guitarist known to the pair called Lloyd Grant. Hetfield played bass in the absence of another player. Bringing the tape to Slagel and borrowing the mastering fee of $50 from a mutual friend, John Kornarens, Ulrich determined to build on the success of the Metal Massacre inclusion and asked James if he would consider forming a band with him. Recruiting James' friend Ron McGovney – who couldn't play bass but got James to show him the rudiments for live purposes – the threesome began jamming and a set of covers, primarily by Diamond Head, Saxon and other NWOBHM standards, emerged.

The new band gained some class when a second guitarist, Dave Mustaine, was asked to join. James wasn't willing to sing and play guitar at the same time and wanted Dave to handle both lead and rhythm parts, a task which the precociously talented Mustaine accepted, contributing riffs to the band's small stock of original material while doing so. Led Zeppelin were Mustaine's idols, as he later said: "Houses Of The Holy was my favourite record, or the Beatles' 'White Album'. I would just listen to them and not even realise that I had gone to the turntable to flip the disc. That was just a mind-melding period for me... Led Zeppelin did come through my town once, but this was just after The Song Remains The Same had come out and I thought that they were starting to lose it, so I didn't go. I was just becoming a cocky young guitar player at the time, and I had no idea how much I'd cheated myself."

Ron McGovney took Mustaine's call, explaining: "We put an ad in Recycler saying we wanted a way-out, fast lead guitar player. I answered the phone one day and this guy named Dave was on the phone, and he was just spieling this baloney like I could not believe. Said he had like four Marshall stacks, four BC Rich Biches. But we got him over and he really was a good lead guitar player."

Lars came up with the name Metallica after weak alternatives such as Blitzer and Grinder were rejected: the idea allegedly came from his friend Ron Quintana, who considered the name for a fanzine but settled on a different moniker, Metal Mania.

Metallica's debut gig came on 14 March 1982 at Radio City in Anaheim, and was a disaster. James was too shy to address the crowd and Dave took an eternity to change a broken string. The dispirited band realised that serious efforts were required to hone an acceptably good act and threw themselves into songwriting, assisted by James' slowly-improving guitar skills and Mustaine's already expert talents. Recording a demo, Power Metal, in April 1982, and booking gigs through the summer, the band slowly evolved their act and after Metal Massacre appeared on 14 June on Slagel's own label, Metal Blade, began to make a name for themselves.

A better and more widely distributed demo entitled No Life 'Til Leather was recorded in July and was immediately copied nationally and internationally, with the metal scene energised by James' clean, precise picking and Mustaine's devastating leads. Journalist Bob Nalbandian, a key mover on the West Coast, says of the No Life demo: "No Life 'Til Leather really struck a chord in San Francisco. I know Ron Quintana had a bunch of friends who were into Venom so much, who were like gods on the underground scene... NLTL was the ultimate demo tape back then. They were one of the first US bands to have an impact with a demo. Before that, no-one got reviews from a demo tape. But in the UK and Europe all these bands like Sweet Savage and Mercyful Fate would put out demos and we would trade them. Blitzkrieg, Satan, Deep Machine and all the Neat Records bands did it too. Metallica got wind of that and put one out. But no-one had thought a demo tape could make a band

big. Bands would put out demos because they couldn't afford to do records… All these key people had the tape, because we sent it out to KJ Doughton in Oregon, and Aardschok magazine in Holland, and Bernard Doe at Metal Forces in England."

By August '82 Metallica had realised that with the performing, writing and recording skills of Dave, James and Lars all approaching expert level, Ron had to go. As it happened, Slagel had already told them about a bassist called Cliff Burton, a fantastically talented player in a band called Trauma. As Cliff later told journalist Harald Oimoen: "Trauma went down to LA and did some stuff. While in LA, Lars and James saw us and decided that they would like to have me in their band. And so they started getting ahold of me and calling me, and I came to their shows here when they played Frisco. And eventually Trauma started to… annoy me… a couple of different ways, so I said, later… It was starting to get a little commercial in different ways, just different general musical attitudes that I found annoying".

After a few shows in San Francisco, where thrash metal had taken hold far more quickly than in the glam-metal-obsessed Los Angeles, Metallica asked Cliff to join them – and he relocated there permanently. A Bay Area show demonstrated how committed the San Fran audience were, reinforcing their decision. The Bay has gone down in history ever since as one of the most fertile hotspots for heavy metal: as Andy Sneap, producer and guitarist with British thrash metal band Sabbat, recalled: "When I was younger I always had this picture in my mind of the Bay Area as this huge scene which was going off, and then later when I was working out there I realised that it's more a collective group of people who all knew each other and were trying to out-shred each other. So it wasn't as big as the magazines hyped it up to be. Really, it was a few individuals who were keeping the whole thing going. They've all been in each other's bands. There was a lot of competition in the Bay Area at the time, rather like the Swedish death metal thing which is going off now".

A show at The Old Waldorf on 29 November saw local thrash metal act Exodus in support, and was the first time that Metallica met their future guitarist, Exodus founder Kirk Hammett. The show was recorded for the Live Metal Up Your Ass demo. The next night was Ron's last gig with Metallica: he was immediately replaced by Burton and songwriting sessions began in earnest.

Things moved fast and in January 1983 the band came into contact with Jon Zazula, a record store owner across the country in New York, who had heard Live Metal Up Your Ass and was interested in managing the band. An epic, and much-documented journey followed, with Metallica renting a van and driving their equipment all the way across America. The journey was made more arduous by Mustaine, whose drinking was getting out of hand.

As Zazula explained: "They needed some money to get here, which was very tight for us in those days – we weren't wealthy people by any means. So we sent them 1500 dollars to come across. They got a one-way rental: a U-Haul van and a truck. Literally, they had two drivers and they slept in the back with all their gear, and they delivered themselves to my front door. It was basically, well, we're here – what do we do next?"

James added that on the journey, Mustaine had been drunk while driving the U-Haul: "If there had been a smash, we could have all got killed". He told Thrasher: "All of a sudden, a straight drive out to New York in a U-Haul. There were five of us and we had a mattress in the back… Get in the back. Slam. You're shut in. We'd never been out of California, and we got there to find out we were having some real problems with Dave's attitude. He couldn't really handle being away from home, or something… we knew it couldn't go on like that, so we started looking at other stuff".

On arrival in NYC, Lars and James informed Zazula that a new guitarist would be recruited, and after a show supporting Venom, asked Dave to leave. Meanwhile, Hammett had been approached to join in his place and was already on the way to New York.

Mustaine had never been the easiest person to live with, once coming to blows with Hetfield. As he explained, "I was dealing drugs to keep myself afloat, because my mom had moved out. It had become a way of life for me, and when I would do a concert people knew I was gone, so they'd jump in through my window and steal my stuff. There are only so many places you can hide something in a house, and usually it was an insider, people who had been there. So I had dogs to protect my merchandise."

One of his dogs jumped on Ron's car: "I took one of them with me up to rehearsal one day and the dog put her paws on the bass player's car. I don't know if it scratched it or left paw-prints, or you know, put a fuckin' dent in the car, I don't know." Hetfield objected to this: "James kicked the dog and we started arguing," said Mustaine. "Push led to shove and I hit him, and I regret it. If I had the chance to do it all over again, I would not have brought the dog."

Ron McGovney told the same story differently: "Dave had come over to my house on a Sunday afternoon and he brought his two pit bull puppies. I think I was in the shower at the time; anyway, Dave let the dogs loose and they were jumping all over my car scratching the shit out of it, I had a rebuilt '72 Pontiac LeMans. And James came out and said 'Hey Dave, get those fuckin' dogs off of Ron's car!' And Dave said, 'What the fuck did you say? Don't you talk that way about my dogs!' Then they started fighting and it spilled into the house, and when I came out of the shower I see Dave punch James right across the

17

mouth and he flies across the room, so I jumped on Dave's back and he flipped me over onto the coffee table. And then James gets up and yells to Dave, 'You're out of the fuckin' band! Get the fuck out of here!' So Dave loaded all his shit up and left all pissed off. The next day he comes back crying, pleading 'Please let me back in the band'."

As well as being a little easier to deal with than Dave, Kirk was a classic metal player, explaining: "I loved Jimi Hendrix, Kiss, Aerosmith, and ZZ Top, and I felt that if I learned how to play their music, I'd become closer to them, I'd be unlocking some sort of mystery. When you learn how to play someone's music, it answers questions on a musical level, but it remains a mystery on other levels. I just felt that if I made their music, I'd be making a connection to them."

But Mustaine told Nalbandian, "When I joined that band they only had one song, 'Hit The Lights'. James did not write that song, [an old guitarist] Hugh Tanner wrote it... [as well as] the song 'Motorbreath'... I wrote the most songs on that whole fuckin' album! I wrote four of them, James wrote three, and Hugh Tanner wrote two!" He added, "I'm just wondering what Metallica are gonna do when they run out of my riffs", and introduced his new band, Megadeth, with the words, "I thought I'd have a helluva lot harder time coming up with something better, but this is three times faster, more advanced and a helluva lot heavier!" Mustaine also told Bob that "I already smashed James in the mouth one time, and Lars is scared of his own shadow", and "Kirk is a 'Yes' man... 'Yes, Lars, I'll do Dave's leads'; 'Yes, James, I'll play this'... James played all the rhythm on that album and Cliff wrote all Kirk's leads, so it shows you they're having a lot of trouble with this 'New Guitar God'."

Despite Dave's malevolence, the new band gelled immediately, but were asked to leave the Zazulas' house (where they had been partying rather too hard) and move into a rehearsal space. Their new home was grim. As Zazula remembers: "We put them into this terrible, terrible, terrible, legendary place called the Music Building. They shared a rehearsal room with Anthrax, but they actually slept in a terrible area. It was like a storage place, it was a part of the building where they had all the rubbish. It was a terrible scene, but I had really no choice. I didn't know what I was getting myself into either!" Kirk remembered it too: "The Music Building was something else. I found a piece of foam on the ground, and I used that as a mattress to put my sleeping bag on. The people that owned it didn't put any time into it. The place had no hot water. I remember washing my hair in the sink using cold water, it was brutal".

Scott Ian of Anthrax explains that he and his bandmates used to help Metallica out: "They had no money, they had nowhere to go, so we pretty much went out of our way to help them out in any way we could. We brought them to our houses to shower, and we gave them a refrigerator and a toaster oven so they could cook the hot dogs that they were eating cold. We just hung out as much as possible".

Meanwhile, Jon and his wife Marsha began making inquiries into possible record deals for Metallica. Meeting with no success, they decided to fund the recording, manufacture and release of the record by themselves on a home-based label called Megaforce. As Jon said: "Marsha and I are miraculous at moving one penny from here to over there. We did whatever we had to do. Second mortgages. We put our life up, we literally put our life on hold to do this. It was sink or swim… It was horrible. Some of those days were the worst days of my life. My neck was constantly in a noose. And we'd just had a baby, you know? It was like the Christians in the Colosseum walking out to the lions! We decided to do it ourselves, and fuck everybody. We just said, to hell with what people say, we're gonna do it. And people thought we were mad. We just did it."

In May 1983 Metallica travelled upstate to record their debut album, produced by Paul Curcio. The original plan was to call it Metal Up Your Ass, but distributors objected and in revenge against this Kill 'Em All was chosen. Two months later the LP was released by Megaforce in the US and Music For Nations in the UK, with whom Zazula had struck a deal. The album was a massive influence on the developing extreme metal scene, with Thomas Fischer, at the time with Hellhammer and soon to be with Celtic Frost, saying: "There was one major instance in which Metallica were an important inspiration on our own early work. That was the area of precision. Being still somewhat new on our instruments, we were much more sloppy in the execution of our music, and the American bands which flooded the underground scene by means of demos, singles and compilation albums seemed a million times more professional in that respect. We of course never reached that level of precision, but the standard was set and remained firmly engraved in our consciousness".

Although songs like 'Phantom Lord' and 'Jump In The Fire' featured devil-worshipping lyrics, it's interesting to note that Metallica abandoned the Satanic angle completely after these songs, perhaps realising that the approach wasn't for them. Slayer and many other thrash acts would take the theme to another level, but they too realised after a year or two that no-one really took it seriously and that the whole devilry thing was best left to the much more committed black metal scene, which was up and running by the following year. A high point of Kill 'Em All was 'Seek And Destroy': more enjoyable in concert than on record, 'Seek…'"s importance to Metallica's career can be measured in the confidence it gave James as a frontman when he performed it. "What the fuck do you call that?" he would yell at the crowd after each enormous yell of "Seek and destroy!", urging them to greater efforts. Live, this song is something to behold.

June 1983 saw Metallica touring with British metal trio Raven: the Raven album at the time was entitled All for One and so the jaunt was dubbed the Kill 'Em All For One tour. Songwriting sessions followed and the rest of the year was taken up with the occasional gig and rehearsals back in San Francisco. Gigs with Armored Saint in November 1983 were followed by drinking marathons, as James told Kerrang!: "Well, as usual, we'd spent hours and hours in the bar and then we decided to booze it up with Armored Saint, so we went up to [Saint bassist] Joey Vera's room and drank all his beer. We were all getting really ripped and started throwing bottles out the window. They were smashing and it sounded really neat. But that soon got boring, so I threw Joey's black and red leather jacket out and it landed in the pool, which luckily had its cover on. So we went down to get it and on the way back up to the tenth floor I decided to open the elevator doors between floors... we then got stuck for half an hour and everyone is like freaking out and I started shouting, get us the fuck out of here! We finally get up to the tenth floor and by now I'm pretty [mad] so I see this fire extinguisher hanging on the wall. So I kinda took it down and started squirting people with it – all this CO2 or some kinda shit was comin' out of it".

A pivotal moment came in February 1984, when Metallica came to Europe for the first time as a band. Touring with Venom through Switzerland, Germany, France and Belgium, then finishing with the Aardschok Festival in Zwolle, Holland, the band were supported by Music For Nations, who released the Jump In The Fire EP to promote the shows. Several notable UK writers met the band for the first time at this point. Metal Forces writer Bernard Doe said: "I first met up with Lars Ulrich the day after he arrived in the UK ahead of the band's first European tour in 1984 with Venom, and over the next 10 years I interviewed him several times. It was funny, because after each interview in

those early days Lars would nearly always call me up a couple of days later and ask me to change or leave some comments out that he had made about an individual or another band. He was very conscious of not upsetting anyone back then. I've always got on well with Lars and I think that we had a mutual respect for one another. He spent a lot of time in Europe, and in particular London, when Metallica were not touring. There were many drunken nights out on the town, and I have the photos to prove it! Back then he never seemed to pay for anything. I never ever saw him once buy a drink. He also had a habit of turning up in Shades record store just as they were about to close, so he could blag some free records. He was always asking about my New Wave Of British Heavy Metal record collection. I remember he was after a copy of a Trespass 7" single. It wasn't a particularly rare record, but I had a copy with a picture sleeve which he didn't have. He actually agreed to trade an official Metallica RIAA gold album award for my copy of the Trespass single! A great deal as far as I was concerned, except he never did fulfil his side of the bargain. James Hetfield occasionally came along with Lars. He loved a drink too (not to mention female Italian tourists!) but was pretty arrogant and could be quite obnoxious at times. I interviewed James just before the 'Black Album' was released, by which time he had mellowed a whole lot".

Another noted writer, Borivoj Krgin, also met Metallica, and recalled: "My impression was pretty much the same as everyone else's: Lars was cocky, arrogant and incredibly self-assured. From the perspective of an interviewer, he was great in the sense that he would just keep talking and talking, regardless of what question he was asked. But as you can imagine, that kind of cocky attitude turned a lot of people off, and he still remains unquestionably the single most hated person in that band precisely for that reason. Kirk was always very down-to-earth and nice, and seemed to be very unpretentious, and the same goes for [later bassist] Jason. Both of them seemed to have good heads on their shoulders and didn't let the band's immense success get in the way of their perception of reality. I met James a few times over the years, and I thought he was a very guarded person who probably didn't let very many people – if anyone – get close to him. He was friendly enough, but he definitely gave off the vibe that he didn't necessarily want people to approach him, if you know what I mean. He definitely exuded a more 'stand-offish' vibe than Jason and Kirk, and it makes much more sense now, especially with all the things he has been talking about in interviews. Having said that, I always appreciated the fact that he seemed to be true to himself and didn't go out of his way to be friendly to everyone simply because people expected him or wanted him to be that way. In essence, he seemed pretty tormented inside and came across like he had a lot of demons to deal with".

Recording sessions followed, this time at the entirely more professional environment of Sweet Silence Studios, Copenhagen, in Lars' home country. Appearing on 27 June 1984, Ride The Lightning was a cohesive, stunning piece of work, establishing Metallica as the obvious leaders of the thrash metal scene and remaining a classic to this day. In November the Creeping Death EP appeared, which featured Blitzkrieg and Diamond Head covers on the B-side, and the following summer Metallica scored much British publicity with a slot at the famous Monsters of Rock festival at Donington between Ratt and Bon Jovi. James uttered the now-famous words, "If you came here to see spandex, eye makeup, and the words 'Oh baby' in every fuckin' song, this ain't the fuckin' band!"

A step up occurred when Metallica quit out of their management contract with Zazula and their record deal with his label Megaforce, signing up with the giant management organisation Q-Prime (which also handled Def Leppard) and the equally huge Elektra, a subsidiary of Warners. Kirk explained: "We looked at each [offer] individually and it seemed from what we saw that Elektra was better. Even though other offers were financially better, Elektra had a reputation for leaving complete artistic freedom with their acts. They had acts in the past, like the Doors, the Velvet Underground, the Stooges... it was a pretty liberal label. They had a reputation for trying out new things that were pretty experimental at the time".

James continued: "Right then there were [a lot of] bands being signed, snatched up on major labels. All the major labels were saying, oh, metal's like the new thing, get in on the money right now. They're still doing it. Elektra only had Mötley Crüe and Dokken, and all these other labels had many more. We'd be say, third on the list of so-called metal bands with Elektra, so we'd get at least some support. Instead of signing with Atlantic where there were 10 metal bands... There wasn't a clutter of metal on that label, so we figured we'd do something to get some support". Kirk added, not for the last time in Metallica's career, that they had received some criticism for 'selling out' by signing with a major company, but that "It didn't affect us at all. We basically didn't give a fuck. We were going to stick to our guns".

Sticking to their guns seemed to be the best possible approach, judging by the results of a recording session over three months in the autumn of 1985, once again with producer Flemming Rasmussen at Copenhagen's Sweet Silence facility. When the phenomenal Master Of Puppets was released in March 1986, it was a revelation – a melodic but aggressive, technical but memorable album of killer tunes that has since gone down as the finest thrash metal album ever recorded, alongside Slayer's Reign In Blood. A key change in the band's commercial status came after Q-Prime secured them the support slot on Ozzy Osbourne's 1986 tour, which exposed them to millions of fans and was their last tour as a supporting act.

But mid-1986 would be a dark time for the band. First James broke his wrist while skateboarding before a gig in Evansville, Indiana: for the rest of the tour, roadie John Marshall (also of Metal Church) stood in on rhythm guitar. As Marshall recalls, he preferred to stand offstage where the crowd couldn't see him: "The first six gigs I played in '86 were opening for Ozzy, and I stood off to the side of the stage where the audience couldn't see me. James would introduce me after about two songs or so. The rest of the gigs that year were in Europe and the UK. I was sort of off to the side where the audience could see me, but kind of in the background. After a few gigs Cliff would motion for me to stand more on stage, and eventually I was onstage every night. I remember the crowd reaction usually being positive. After all, it was still Metallica, just with one more guy onstage... the hard part was trying to match the vibe and intensity of his guitar playing. I knew how to play the riffs and song arrangements OK, but getting the feel right was difficult. It was also hard because the rest of the band follows his voice and guitar onstage. I wasn't used to that type of situation. I think I was more worried about what the rest of the band thought, than what the audience thought... The first time I played I literally had to learn the songs overnight, so I didn't have much time to think about it. I remember feeling really excited, a little stunned that they had actually asked me, and a little nervous".

Much more tragically, a coach crash in Sweden at about 6am on 27 September changed the band's outlook forever. Travelling along a road between the Scandinavian cities of Stockholm and Copenhagen, the driver lost control of the vehicle.

Marshall, who was on board, explains: "Apparently the bus drifted off to the right side of the road, and the driver steered left to correct. As he did this, the back end of the bus spun out to the right. While this was happening, I remember waking up, being

28

bounced out of the bunk because the tyres were 'chattering' as the bus skidded.

"By the time it stopped, the bus was on the right side of the road, facing the other direction. As it slid into the right shoulder of the road, it caught the gravel and tipped onto its right side. When the bus tipped, the two rows of bunks collapsed together, trapping guys underneath".

John then climbed out of the bus. "I remember crawling out of the door, which was now facing upwards (it was a UK coach, with its entry on the left side) and jumping to the ground. I remember sitting out on the ground, waiting for help, just stunned at being awakened this way, and trying to take it all in. Bobby Schneider, the tour manager, was still inside the bus, helping to get the guys out".

The bus had thrown the sleeping Cliff Burton through a window and onto the road, before falling on him and killing him instantly. "I saw the bus lying right on him," said James in 1993. "I saw his legs sticking out. I freaked. The bus driver, I recall, was trying to yank the blanket out from under him to use for other people. I just went, 'Don't fucking do that!' I already wanted to kill the guy. I don't know if he was drunk or if he hit some ice. All I knew was, he was driving and Cliff wasn't alive any more."

The dazed band were taken to the local police station, where the driver was routinely arrested (he was later freed) and the remaining personnel could attempt to recover. The tour was cancelled and the band flew home two days later, attending Cliff's funeral some time later.

They didn't sit around for long, as Kirk later explained: "Right after the accident happened, we individually decided that the best way to get rid of all our frustrations would be to hit the road and get all the anxiety and frustrations out on stage, where they should go. They should go toward a positive thing

like that. We were very traumatised, and felt a lot of emotional distress over the situation... The worst thing we could do is just sit in our room and sulk over the matter and wallow in our pity. The more you think about it, the deeper you sink. We each thought individually, we have to keep on going, we have to work because it wouldn't be fair to Cliff to just stop. Also if he were alive for some reason or another and like, y'know, he couldn't play bass, he wouldn't tell us to stop. That's the way he would've felt. He would've wanted us to go on." James told MTV a similar story: "The last thing Cliff would've wanted us to do was quit. He'd be the first one to kick us in the ass and make us wake up".

Back in America, Brian Slagel was helping Metallica find another bass player. Auditioning Les Claypool (later of Primus) and many others, Lars, James and Kirk weren't exactly flooded with decent candidates – but Brian knew a possible player. "Apparently a couple of other people Lars spoke to had thought of Flotsam And Jetsam and told him yeah, that guy's really good," said Slagel. "So we arranged for their bass player, Jason Newsted, to fly up to San Fran to audition. I called Jason and said, I don't want to get you too excited... what would you think about possibly auditioning for the Metallica gig? He was freaking out, saying, are you kidding me? They're like my favourite band of all time! I think he was more nervous than anything else – like, really? This is really happening? And I was like, yeah! You should definitely do it. It was hard because Flotsam And Jetsam was his band. But then again Metallica was his favourite band, so it didn't take too much arm-twisting to get him to go up there".

On 28 October – just a month after Cliff's death – Jason auditioned with Metallica, having learned all their songs beforehand. When the three of them asked him what song he would like to play, he said "any one you like". He was readily accepted into the band after a drinking session at a venue called Tommy's Joint, with the words "Welcome to Metallica".

There was little time to wait around, as Metallica had Californian gigs and their first Japanese tour lined up. Jason's first gig with Metallica was in support of Metal Church at The Country Club in Reseda, followed by a set at Jezabelle's in Anaheim and the flight East. Immediately, Lars, James and Kirk began teasing him with pranks and practical jokes that – at first – he laughed off. As he told Rolling Stone: "It was a test all the time – windups from everyone to see if I could cut it. Everybody would go down to the bar to have sushi and sake for days and charge it to my room. We'd go to take pictures at the temples, and they'd all get in one taxi and make me ride by myself."

However, the hazing continued, and Jason realised that he was part of a band in crisis: "This went on for a year. If I was going to buckle, they had to know. I took it and that was that." The band later acknowledged that much of this treatment was simply down to them taking out their grief and shock at Cliff's death on the new recruit.

By 1987 the band had – superficially at least – stabilised, and recordings were underway for a release that would introduce Jason to the Metallica fanbase. When the five-track (four tracks in the UK) The $5.98 EP: Garage Days Re-Revisited was released on 10 August, it was an immediate hit, showcasing Jason's fat bass sound and dexterous style and acting as a suitable precursor to the live shows that summer. In December that year Metallica released a VHS called Cliff 'Em All – a collection of grainy Burton footage that is essential viewing to this day.

And so the post-Cliff line-up of Metallica found a foothold. The next step up the ladder of fame was a slot on the summer 1988 Monsters Of Rock Festival (as distinct from the UK Donington event) with Van Halen in support and others including Scorpions, Kingdom Come and Dokken. Metallica stole the show on most dates, partying harder than ever before and taking intermediate time out to mix their latest recording sessions, a new album entitled ...And Justice For All. Lars loved the MOR tour, telling Rolling Stone: "It was fucking great. It was '88, right before ...And Justice for All came out. We were at the bottom, sandwiched between Kingdom Come and Dokken. Basically, at that time, we used to start drinking when we woke up. We'd get the gig over by three o'clock, and then we'd have eight or nine hours to drink. It was awesome. This was our first exposure to big crowds, like, 50,000 people every day. Well, we were just drunk basically all the time. Girls knew we were part of the tour and wanted to fuck us, but at the same time we could blend in with the crowd. There's a point where you end up sitting in your dressing room because there's 14 layers of security. Back then it was like, who gives a shit? Let's have another rum and Coke and go back in the audience and see what's happening. There are pictures of us at the top of Tampa Stadium with our pants off, flashing everybody. It's four o'clock in the afternoon and we're already drunk off our asses. The not-giving-a-fuck meter was peaking".

Indeed. In September 1988 Justice was released, scoring mixed reactions despite its exquisite arrangements and catchy, satisfyingly dark tunes. The main problem for most fans was its mix, executed by the Steve Thompson and Michael Barbiero mixing team according to Lars and James' instructions. Jason's bass parts were mixed out almost entirely, leaving the record dominated by James' huge, cold guitar sound.

Newsted was disappointed by the results but kept quiet about it for many years, only opening up about the issues a decade later. As he recalled, the recording sessions themselves started badly, perhaps because the original producer, Mike Clink, had been fired to be replaced by Rasmussen: "They're juggling producers. There's no order. And no authority to say, we need this producer doing this, at this time, to record that, to make that happen. Even though we had the money. Even though we had the support of the label. Even though we had a nice studio. And all that kinda thing. None of that was in order... I stepped in with an assistant engineer and I had my same gear that I would just play on the stage. There was no time taken about 'you place this microphone here, and this one will sound better than that, should we mix it with the DI, should we use this bass instead of that bass, should we get that tonality, should you use a pick, should you use your fingers? Any of the things that I know now, that make a really good bass sound. You plug in, you play the song. I could play 'em standing on my head with my eyes closed, any of those songs. I rehearsed those songs up the ass. Right?"

He added: "So I go in and I knock 'em out. Basically, doubling James' guitar parts, because that's the kind of bass player I was then. Lars and James weren't around to say, you should try that there instead of that there. Or a real producer or a manager, or anybody saying, that's OK. I'd go in and record three or four songs in a day or an afternoon. I'd just sit there and knock it out. And there'd be mistakes and whatever. I'd just play it and that would be that. And OK, you did good – bye! Usually nowadays I'd take one day per song. That's what I do on albums. So I allow myself to get in early, to get the sound you want, you go and you record all day to get that fit, that's what I allow myself. Now some guys take a lot longer, some guys take less time. But back then, I didn't even know anything about that shit. Just played it and that was that, right?"

On top of this, Metallica were performing on the Van Halen tour while mixing was going on: "So then we get the offer to go on Monsters Of Rock in the summer, OK? And by the time they've bopped Mike Clink out of the producer's seat, and there's a void, and then Flemming comes in, my stuff's already on tape and put in the back and forgotten. We get to the mixing

stage and no-one is chosen for the mix. Still no order in that either. We go on this tour with Van Halen and Scorpions – the guys who invented partying, piles of powder here and there and all that shit... that was the first taste for us of dipping your foot in the actual scene of rock and roll, you know. So we're doing a few shows a week with those guys on that special festival – and on the days that we aren't, James and Lars are flying to Bearsville, New York, to mix it with these two other cats [Thompson and Barbiero], right, that I never met in my life, and I had no idea at all.

"So they're partying, travelling back and forth, getting no sleep, going there early with kind of an attitude about the bass – it's not Cliff, and yadda yadda – and they go in and tell the [mixers], get the bass just where you can hear it, and then take it down a half a DB. Then turn all the frequency up on the guitars, and all that stuff. And then try to make the bass drum to fill in all the space so it can be all percussive, and all that kind of thing. And that is why it is... I've learned a lot from that. I was so in the dirt, I was so disappointed when I heard the final mix, I basically blocked it out, like people do with shit. We were firing on all cylinders, and shit was happening. I was just rolling with it and going forward. What was I gonna do, say we gotta go remix it, when we were down to the last minutes with people saying, we gotta say when, we gotta say when? And all that bullshit. Now, if you were to ask them, now that they have time and they're fathers, you know, life, maturity... they would go, fuck. Whoops! They would say it right to your face".

In late 1988 Metallica began the extensive Damaged Justice Tour 88-89 in Budapest, Hungary, before releasing a professionally filmed video for the single, 'One'. Early in 1989 it seemded that the industry had finally woken up to Metallica, nominating them for a Grammy in the heavy metal category. Amazingly, folk-rockers Jethro Tull won, leading Metallica to add stickers to the sleeve of later pressings of ...AJFA which read 'Grammy Award LOSERS'. The following year the band did in fact win a Grammy for Best Metal Performance, for 'One', and thanked Tull in their speech for not releasing any material that year.

1989 and 1990 passed in a blur for Metallica, who kept their profile relatively low, only releasing a cover of Queen's 'Stone Cold Crazy' for an Elektra anniversary album, which would net them another Grammy in early 1991. Much of 1990 was spent in rehearsals and recording for the next album – in fact, the band were in the One On One studio in North Hollywood with a new producer, Bob Rock, for several months from October. Rock had been chosen for his track record with Mötley Crüe and The Cult among others, and was thought likely to bring about radical changes to the band's sound...

But no-one had foreseen quite how radical. When the video for a new song, 'Enter Sandman', was premiered on 30 July 1991, fans were astounded at how mainstream and polished the new sound was, with the song basically a fist-pounding heavy metal anthem and full to the brim with a big, big bass sound – worlds away from the thin frequencies and complex arrangements of the last album, three years earlier. A huge tour was set to begin on 1 August, with the album – the self-titled Metallica, with a pure black sleeve, Spinal Tap-style – on the way on the 12th. Some shops opened at one minute past midnight on that day, so great was the demand and the hype that Elektra had placed behind what would be universally known as the 'Black Album'.

The tour, which would roll on with scarcely a break for the best part of three years, was full of highlights. One was a show in Moscow at the invitation of the Russian Prime Minister, which attracted 500,000 people and seemed somehow to embody a new future for the country, which had recently seen the fall of the Soviet Union. Another was the Concert For Life, a 20 April

1992 show at the Wembley Stadium in London dedicated to the late Freddy Mercury.

In August that year James was seriously burned by pyrotechnics on stage in Montreal, Canada, and the long-suffering (but presumably well-paid) John Marshall was recruited for guitar duties as a result. Three months later Metallica jammed with all four members of Diamond Head on stage in Birmingham, and two videos, A Year And A Half In The Life Of Metallica Parts 1 & 2, were released, taking the viewer through the arduous Black Album recording and beyond.

All this live activity was chronicled at the end of 1993 by a three-CD, two-video box set called Live Shit: Binge And Purge, that retailed at a high price but delivered serious value, with a book and various mementos inside. Some critics accused the band of exploiting their fans, but James responded: "If we put these things out separately over the years, it would cost the same amount of money, maybe more. It seems that other bands put crap out because 'wow, we need money' or something, and this is absolutely not that! It's chock full of various stuff, more than enough. There's stuff in the book we shouldn't even be showing people, some of the faxes and stuff. It is way over the top and yeah, I think it's great. Nothing's really stood out like this does, as far as live albums or videos are concerned".

Lars added: "What we're doing is saying, here it is, take it or leave it. And the reason it costs $89.95 is not so we and Elektra can walk away with big fat bank accounts, it's basically to cover the fucking costs of about two and a half million bucks. Our management did a survey and discovered that this is the most expensive packaging anybody has ever put together. You've got everything in there, nine hours of music, a 72-page book, backstage passes, stencil, keys to our houses... so fuck, take it or leave it!

"I think it's turned into a great way of getting the last three and a half years out of our systems. Now the slate really is completely clean. We wrote the album, made the album, toured the album and here's the documentation of the album's music on the road. Now we can take our nine months or whatever off and start with a clean slate. Everything about this tour is gone. It will enable us to completely let go of everything from the last few years, and when we begin to approach the next album we can do so without any lingering, left-over baggage... It's our first attempt at a live package, and it's definitely the right time in our career to do this. It's also the right time for us to take a step away from everything for however long. And it's the perfect way to leave our hardcore fans with something to listen to while we're away".

James: "I wanted to hang onto [the video tapes] for a long time, because it was the only properly shot old shit we had. It had a lot of stuff that we – myself anyway – didn't really wanna get rid of right now. We'd always talked of it being something that would come out 10 years down the line, like, wow, here's some vintage crap that's never been seen and, wow, it's on proper film, that sort of thing. But as we started watching it, we found that it was pretty alright stuff, and we agreed to just get it all out now so as it doesn't look really out of place later". With ironic prescience, he concluded: "If we'd held on, it could've been a situation where we're rockin' along and this thing comes out 10 years later, people see it and start saying, hey... they used to be good! Hahaha".

After six months off, the rest of 1994 was taken up with the Shit Hits The Sheds tour, which saw guest spots from members of Danzig, Judas Priest and others. Two new songs from the yet-to-be-released next album, '2 x 4' and 'Devil's Dance', were played at the London Astoria for members of the fan club. Memorable shows followed at the 'Coldest Show On Earth' in Arctic Canada and at Motörhead singer Lemmy's 50th birthday party at the Whiskey A Go-Go. From December 1995 to February 1996 Metallica were ensconced in the Plant studio in Sausalito, California, with Bob Rock once more. Some wondered if the new record would emulate the anthemic, stripped-down Black Album or return to the thrash roots of yore. Once again, the results would surprise everybody.

Emerging in May 1996, Metallica played local shows in San Francisco and shot a video for a new single, 'Until It Sleeps', before embarking on a promotional spree for the new album, Load, which was released wordwide on 4 June. Explaining the use of Rock once more, James laughed: "Well, we figured we got to know Bob really well on the last recording. We didn't really make him completely insane, so we had to come back and finish the job. He had a couple of brain cells left that we had to tweak. I think after the Black Album, we told each other that we were never going to work together again. But time heals all, and we never really could see this record with someone else. It was always him, we knew he'd be back. This time there was no intimidation factor and there was no 'you can't tell me what to do' bullshit. All that petty crap was out of the way, it was more like a friendly set of ears in the studio... Bob tends to help us dig deeper. We tell him what we're after and he tries to help us achieve that".

There was no escaping the fact that Load was a weak album – see the track-by-track analysis for in-depth detail – but Metallica fought hard to promote it innovatively, performing a webcast (one of the new internet technology's first such events, even though with the ubiquitous dial-up web access few could access it), staging a fan competition of enormous scale and headlining the US Lollapalooza festival. This last was an unusual move for an event which had scraped the barrel dry of so-called 'alternative' acts: but then Metallica were in a strange place in 1996, with an overhaul of their image as drastic as their sound. All four men had short haircuts; Lars, Kirk and Jason (but thankfully not the hulking Hetfield) were experimenting with eyeliner; Kirk had embraced the body-piercing and tattoos trend; and all wore a variety of strange, semi-cool, semi-dorky garb that was a universe away from the trainers and denim standard of the previous decade.

A tour commenced in September – not to the same exhausting scale as the Black Album tour, much to the band-members' relief – punctuated by TV and award-show slots that served to confirm the band's enormous stature on the international rock scene. On 13 November, for example, the band performed 'Wasting My Hate', a solo acoustic version of 'Mama Said' and 'King Nothing' on BBC2's Later With Jools Holland (thankfully the host didn't attempt his usual trick of playing boogie-woogie piano along with them) and played 'So What?' at the MTV Europe Video Awards show. The latter song – a classic UK punk staple from The Anti-Nowhere League, complete with F and C words – was a slightly controversial choice, as James explained: "We needed to wake people up at the show! We felt it was a little boring, and we had been daring each other to do that for years".

A year of shows and promotion segued neatly into a repeat performance for the next album, announced as the second part of the Load sessions. Titled Reload, the record was launched with a free show on 11 November, at a venue suggested by over 120,000 fans, who had called a free number to suggest a suitable location. The CoreStates Arena parking lot in South Philadelphia was the place chosen, and despite massive (and unnecessary) protests from neighbouring residents and businesses, the show was a great success. The Philadelphia Inquirer reported that 'The Million Decibel March', as it was dubbed, was "part burlesque show, part rugby match, and hearing-loss loud. The band was profane on stage and charming before the show. Police pronounced the fans better behaved than a Philadelphia Eagles crowd. And neighbors who feared the worst from the self-styled Loudest Band in the World complained more about the sound from the news choppers circling overhead."

Reload was even poorer than Load, but Metallica appeared not to care, pulling out all the stops for a video shoot for the lead single 'The Memory Remains' – a spectacular stunt epic filmed at the Van Nuys airport – performing on NBC's Saturday Night Live and playing a free show at London superclub the Ministry Of Sound. The usual world tour followed.

It seemed that nothing could stop the band's endless creativity, even if the results weren't always up to the standard of their classic 1980s material. Despite interruptions (both positive and negative) such as Lars becoming a father in August '98 and Jason being struck by a glass bottle thrown on stage on 5 September (James: "We're here to give it all we got, but I don't understand why we have to watch out for shit thrown at

us during the show. I hope they find that fucker who did it"),
plans were laid for a new album, with recording commencing
the day after the last tour show in San Diego. The idea was to
release an album of covers called Garage, Inc., with the first
disc comprising new recordings and the second a round-up
of all the cover versions that Metallica had recorded to date
– and to this end the band executed a plethora of photo and
video shoots, press and studio sessions, all the ingredients of
the superstar regime. In October 1998 the band shot a video
with Swedish director Jonas Akerlund (who had also directed
Madonna's 'Ray Of Light' and The Prodigy's 'Smack My
Bitch Up') at Raleigh Studios in Los Angeles for a cover of
Bob Seger's 'Turn The Page'. The following month, they filed
a lawsuit against Amazon.com over a bootleg CD titled Bay
Area Thrashers: The Early Days – a live and demo collection
from the Mustaine era – and the following January they sued
Victoria's Secret and Victoria's Secret Catalogue, citing
trademark infringement, false designation of origin, unfair
competition, and dilution. The lawsuit stated: "Victoria's Secret
manufactures and sells lip pencils bearing the mark Metallica.
The packaging for Victoria's Secret's Metallica lip pencils also
bear the mark Metallica. These lip pencils continue to be sold
by Victoria's Secret throughout the United States." In an ironic
coincidence, at about the same time – according to the industry
trade publication Pollstar – Metallica made $32 million dollars
that year.

In January 1999 the band released a cover of Thin Lizzy's
'Whiskey In The Jar', which had been disliked by critics
but which is actually an excellent take on the traditional
arrangement. The accompanying video saw the band playing
at a party of drunken, nubile females and then destroying the
room they're playing in – something of a departure. A Grammy
Award for 'Better Than You' came the following month, despite

the weakness of the song; more deservedly, the Recording Industry Association of America gave a diamond award for 10 million copies sold of the Black Album. James thanked Rock "for making the big noises extra big".

In April the band set off on tour again, including two gigs at the Berkeley Community Theatre in San Francisco accompanied by the San Francisco Symphony Orchestra, conducted by Michael Kamen (who had arranged strings for the earlier hit, 'Nothing Else Matters'). The tour was full of special-guest appearances, including Pantera's Phil Anselmo onstage in Mexico City for 'Creeping Death', Evan, Billy and Danny from Biohazard, Scott Ian from Anthrax, and Anthony from Merauder on stage for vocals on the "Die, die, die" section of the same song, and King Diamond and Hank Sherman of Mercyful Fate for the 'Mercyful Fate' medley that had appeared on Garage, Inc.. November 1999 saw more orchestral shows in New York and Germany before the release in the same month of S&M, the artfully titled live/orchestral album recorded back in April.

Of the concept, Kirk explained that the idea had come up "because it's a new challenge for us. It breaks the continuity of recording, performing, recording. It's new. The option to record with a symphonic orchestra is a great thing. It is in fact not the first time it's been done, the connection between rock and a symphony orchestra, but when Deep Purple did it, it was different. Because we take old and known songs, and put them up with the orchestra. They did new things, that weren't necessarily received well... It is sophisticated, complex, without compromise. It's a challenge. No-one expected this from us, and we're taking a risk. That in itself is a statement of some kind."

Lars told MTV: "You know, the thing about the symphony stuff... part of what makes it really cool is the fact that it's not something that ends up being sort of overkill. I don't want to go on tour with this record for 100 dates. It's a great thing to be able

to come back to and do once in a while in special situations, you know, 'It's 2002 and we're down in Australia for two weeks, let's go play one with the Sydney Symphony Orchestra,' that type of thing. But to go out and sort of tour it? No, I think that would take away from the specialty vibe of the whole thing".

Writer Bernard Doe recalls: "I spoke to Lars Ulrich backstage after a show in Stockholm in 1993 and we were talking about the success of the Black Album and where the band went from there, and Lars said then that he thought that the band had possibly reached their peak and wasn't too worried if the next album didn't match that success in terms of sales. He cited Deep Purple as a band, past their peak, that just carried on releasing the occasional album and touring every few years, and seemed content if Metallica's future would carry on along those lines. Well, I guess S&M was Metallica's answer to Deep Purple's 1969 Concerto For Group And Orchestra album".

Asked about the S&M shows, Ulrich said: "It's a lot more intense. Nobody probably wants to hear this, but when you're playing your eighth show in Germany in 10 days, sometimes the mind can wander a little. The two shows in Berkeley with the San Francisco Orchestra... that was about as focused as I've ever been onstage, in terms of wanting to hold down our part of it and not screw up and not let the team down. I guess it's one thing, letting a team of four down. Another is letting a team of 108 down... That's what I remember about the two shows: a complete inner focus and really just dealing with my aspect of it and not wondering about the lights or the pretty girl in row three, and really just holding down my end of it more so than ever. That's the ugly truth".

Metallica had taken the decision to hand over four videos to MTV and five songs to radio for broadcasters to play at will: "Here's five songs, radio can play whichever one, and here's four different videos to you guys... Basically it's our refusal to be the ones to decide on something specific. Let somebody else do it".

The millennium came and went with a New Year's Eve show with Ted Nugent in Pontiac, Michigan, and dates with Kid Rock. 'Whiskey In The Jar' scooped a Grammy for Best Hard Rock Performance in February and all seemed to be going smoothly, until a new lawsuit against a company called Napster was announced in April. Metallica's official statement about the action against the internet filesharing program read, "Metallica is suing Napster because we felt that someone had to address this important artistic issue, and we have always been known for taking a leadership role in the fight for artists' rights. We were the first band to sue our record company, Time Warner, for the right to control our future. Rather than allowing the record company or any other corporation to own our recordings and compositions, we chose to fight for (and eventually win) control of our music. This issue is no different. Why is it all of a sudden OK to get music for free? Why should music be free, when it costs artists money to record and produce it?"

The actual suit, from Metallica and co-plaintiffs E/M Ventures and Creeping Death Music, read "[Napster] encourages and enables visitors to its website to unlawfully exchange with others copyrighted songs and sound recordings without the knowledge or permission of Metallica". This immediately raised the wrath of many of the Metallica fanbase, some of whom were keen file-swappers and who answered a 2 May webchat on ArtistDirect. com with anger. When Jason pointed out that the idea behind the lawsuit was "to spearhead some kind of activity within the powers that be – the government – to lay down the laws with the computer, to exercise some kind of control and govern the companies like Napster that steal outright from artists", and Hetfield said, "Metallica has always felt fans are family," a fan retorted with the words "Your family just got a lot smaller".

James also said, "There has to be some laws and guidelines to go by before it gets too out of hand and sucks the life out of musicians who will stop making music… [Napster] is a big machine… The person who invented Napster is an employee of the big machine as we speak". However, Ulrich may have gone too far for some fans when he said "The goal is clear and simple: put Napster out of business," and then "For the doubters out there, Metallica will carry on for the next 20 years… whether you're around for the ride or not, that's your problem, not ours".

Lars emerged as the spokesman on the issue, coming out in several interviews with slightly over-aggressive statements that infuriated many old-school fans. Although his stance was not unreasonable – he was protecting his property, and now that a few years have passed few sensible observers would deny him that – he handled the affair with too many words and too much negativity. For example, he once said "The record company had nothing to do with it whatsoever… we took it upon ourselves, there was never really much in terms of support… I'm quite stunned at the lack of communication and input from the record company" and went on to explain "I don't want to sound too combative here, but you know, when somebody fucks with what we do, we go after them".

He knew of other file-sharing programs – "Are we aware of the Gnutellas and all these other things? Of course we are, but you can only take it one step at a time… Right now, you know, we know what is not right for us, which is Napster" – and that internet distribution could be useful for the future – "We are not stupid, of course we realise the future of getting music from Metallica to the people who are interested in Metallica's music is through the internet. But the question is, on whose conditions, and obviously we want it to be on our conditions" – but may have regretted statements such as "Everything we hear from our technical advisors on a daily basis is that these fucking internet anarchists sit there and go, well they will never be able to stop Freenet [or] Gnutella because there's no central server. Yeah, you want to fucking watch? You want to fucking watch us stop it? You want to fucking see in three months how we can fucking blow your measly little company apart? No problem".

However, he wasn't completely unreasonable, adding: "Napster could have so easily avoided this whole thing. It's like, OK, we have this service, we would like to know if you are interested in being part of it. If we'd said yes, then there's no issue, if we'd said no, then this whole thing would have never... Are we assholes for wanting to get off this service that I was never asked if I wanted to be part of in the first place?" It was not, he emphasised, about cash flow: "Understand one thing: this is not about a lot of money right now, because the money that's being lost right now is really pocket change, OK? It's about the principle of the thing and it's about what could happen if this kind of thing is allowed to exist and run as rampant and out of control for the next five years as it has been for the last six months. Then it can become a money issue. Right now it's not a money issue. I can guarantee you it's costing us tenfold to fight it in lawyers' fees, in lawyers' compensation, than it is for measly little pennies in royalties being lost, that's not what it's about".

It seemed that sound business sense lay at the root of Ulrich's arguments. He explained: "We treat the business with the respect that it deserves, because if you do not respect the business side of it, you can get fucked... the music world is littered with the careers of people who did not pay enough attention to the business side of what they were doing and ended up getting majorly fucked" and added "Record companies will never be completely extinct, for one reason and one reason only, that there will always be a need to develop younger artists,

and record companies will always be able to play a big part of that, because this whole thing about 'I'm a young band, I'm an upstart band, I'm going to put my music on Napster, and then I'm going to become successful?' Fantasy. The only way you you will become successful is by having a publicity and promotion campaign behind you that elevates what you're doing above what your competition is doing".

The statistics spoke for themselves: "When we monitored Napster for 48 hours three weekends ago, we came up with 1.4 million downloads of Metallica music, and there was one, one downloading – one! of an unsigned artist the whole time. You can sit there and talk about how this is great for up-and-coming artists or for unsigned bands, but a big counterargument that nobody gets is, me and you could form a band together, and we could like, make a demo and then we could put it up on Napster. Who is going to give a fuck?... When we go in, and check Napster out, we come up with 1.4 million copyright infringements in 48 hours, this is a different thing than trading cassette tapes with your buddy at school".

The song at the centre of the Napster controversy – 'I Disappear', taken from the forthcoming Mission: Impossible 2 soundtrack, which had been leaked to radio in unfinished form thanks to internet filesharing – was finally released in June. Disappointingly, it was hardly a career classic. A tour began in June but was racked with misfortune – a member of the audience accidentally fell to his death from a high stadium seat, and James injured some discs in his back, requiring make-up shows to be performed – and was punctuated by extra-curricular events such as Kirk joining a protest march in San Francisco against increased rental prices for rehearsal studios in the city. Meanwhile, James guested with Motörhead and the Misfits; Lars was working on a band called Systematic, signed to his new label, The Music Company; and all seemed well until

17 January 2001, when a shock statement came from Metallica that Jason would be leaving the band.

Fans were truly shocked: Jason had been a Metallica member for 14 years and the least likely to protest about anything that bothered him, all through the Load era, the Napster controversy and the endless tours. He quoted a neck injury as the primary reason for leaving – as he said, "I wanted to stay. It was such a big part of me, I always put it first. There's a lot of truth to the physical thing as far as the damage that I'd done to my neck and my spine and stuff... Repetitive motion over the years. The doctors kept telling me that I kept giving myself whiplash over and over and I would never let it heal, it just kept going back. [But] that was one of many reasons. I wasn't confident that I could be the '110% dude' performer that people know me as, and I need to have that. James, where he was in his head space, you know, at that time, with his personal life and different things... the way that he came at it, and all that kind of thing – I understand why. He was having trouble and yet he's always been the protector of the name. He's always been the protector of the integrity of Metallica. That's why Metallica's what it is, one of the main reasons Metallica is what it is. And between Lars' perseverance and James' fuckin' integrity, that's fuckin' it right there, man. And I realise that now. He was protecting the whole thing, right? But you know when you squeeze too hard sometimes, you know that deal?"

It emerged that James was unwilling to let Jason work on other bands or side projects and had forbidden him to do so for years – not out of meanness but out of fear that Metallica might suffer. Jason continued: "That's kinda what happened. Exactly what he didn't want to happen, exactly what he was fighting for the whole time, he actually drove me away, or something. So, I came to realise that after a bit, but also I know that it had to happen – it was meant to happen – the opportunity that they

have now to kick ass and really go for it, man, take the bull by the horns, the next era of Metallica... like, they're in their third decade now and they keep showing people how it's done. And it's a great time to do it – metal's coming back, and who's better to show people how to do it? Some of the stuff I've heard so far – he's got a lot of stuff to write about. He's got a lot to play about."

Officially, Newsted said: "Due to private and personal reasons, and the physical damage that I have done to myself over the years while playing the music that I love, I must step away from the band. This is the most difficult decision of my life, made in the best interest of my family, myself, and the continued growth of Metallica. I extend my love, thanks, and best wishes to my brothers: James, Lars, and Kirk and the rest of the Metallica family, friends, and fans whom have made these years so unforgettable." The rest of the band were supportive to a fault, with James taking the stiff-upper-lip route ("Playing with someone who has such unbridled passion for music will forever be a huge inspiration. On stage every night, he was a driving force to us all, fans and band alike. His connection will never be broken"), Lars overdoing the cheese as usual ("We part ways with Jason with more love, more mutual respect, and more understanding of each other than at any other point in the past. James, Kirk and I look forward to embracing the next chapter of Metallica with both a huge amount of appreciation for the last 14 years with Jason and the excitement of rising to the challenges that lay ahead to make Metallica shine brighter than ever") and Kirk, who was the closest to Jason and genuinely upset by this turn of events, simply saying "Jason is our brother. He will be missed."

Unknown to the band, the line-up change would lead to all-round evolution, as Lars sensed when he said "We're really enjoying each other's company and retouching on things we haven't connected on in a long time. It's a fun and healthy time for us... The best thing about where we're at right now is we don't have anything in front of us. We for once feel a tremendous amount of freedom to basically do whatever we want and whatever comes to us... We put out four records in four years, the last four years of the 90s, and I don't think anybody's particularly missing Metallica... We want to take our time finding the right person to fill in Jason's spot".

Take their time they certainly did: it would be two years before a replacement was announced. Before this, the usual diet of musical activity and celebrity novelty lay ahead, with Lars winning $32,000 for charity on Who Wants To Be A Millionaire in February, James jamming in San Jose with Corrosion Of Conformity, Lars hanging out with ex-Alice In Chains guitarist Jerry Cantrell and the band scooping another Grammy, this time for the S&M version of 'The Call of Ktulu'. The same month saw the 9th US Circuit Court of Appeals judging against Napster at last, leading Metallica to state: "From day one our fight has always been to protect the rights of artists who chose not to have their music exploited without consent. The court's decision validates this right and confirms that Napster was wrong in taking not only Metallica's music but other artists who do not want to be a part of the Napster system and exploiting it without their approval. We are delighted that the Court has upheld the rights of all artists to protect and control their creative efforts. The 9th Circuit Court has confirmed that musicians, songwriters, filmmakers, authors, visual artists and other members of the creative community are entitled to the same copyright protections online that they traditionally have been afforded offline.

"We have never objected to the technology, the internet or the digital distribution of music. All we have ever asked is that artists be able to control how, when and in what form their creativity is distributed through these channels. This is something that Napster has continually refused to do. Now the court has made that decision for them."

More earnest drivel came from Napster founder Shawn Fanning: "Even when we were at odds with Metallica, we always understood that they had the best interests of artists in mind... Metallica brought to the forefront an important artists' rights issue. They have taken a lot of flak for that but have persevered because of their belief that what they're doing is essential to the preservation of their art. Despite the litigation, Metallica's position has been a reflection of their high ideals and their private dealings with Napster have always been gracious. It's time to end the court fight and shake hands. We look forward to gaining Metallica's support and respect as we work to develop Napster into a tool that can be responsive both to artists' needs to communicate their art and the desires of music lovers throughout the world. We're pleased that this chapter is behind us."

Lars expressed a touch of regret as the case finally closed, looking back and summing up: "I've done thousands of interviews, and I feel that the music media, the Rolling Stones of the world, has been very, very biased against us. The hard thing about this issue is that it's not an issue that you can really explain in what's called a soundbite, in one or two sentences. So it has been very frustrating doing 30 to 45 minute interviews with periodicals and so on, and then seeing one sentence being used, or taken out of context or something like that". With a touch of humility, he added: "Certainly in the beginning of this process I said some things that were out of line... I did an interview with the BBC where I said some things about 'yes we will go after the fans directly' or something like that... this has been a learning process for me also".

Despite this promising news, Metallica's world was rocked

for the second time in as many months with the publication of an article in Playboy magazine that saw the band sniping at each other in obvious annoyance. In the light of Newsted's departure the feature was even more revealing, and the band's growing legion of naysayers lapped up the intra-band comments and even speculated that a split was en route.

When Jason discussed his frustration at not being allowed to release any side projects, James pointed out: "When someone does a side project, it takes away from the strength of Metallica. So there is a little ugliness lately. And it shouldn't be discussed in the press". Newsted added: "We're getting really close to some things we shouldn't be talking about". James: "Where would it end? Does he start touring with it? Does he sell T-shirts? Is it his band? That's the part I don't like. It's like cheating on your wife in a way. Married to each other". Asked "So what is Jason supposed to do during the hiatus?", Hetfield responded "I don't fucking know. I'm not his travel agent".

Hammett supported Jason ("James demands loyalty and unity, and I respect that, but I don't think he realises the sequence of events he's putting into play... I think it's morally wrong to keep someone away from what keeps him happy"), but Ulrich seemed not to care, citing domestic issues ("I just can't get caught up in these meltdowns. I've got some issues in my family life, with my wife, that are a little more weighty than, like, whatever James Hetfield and Jason Newsted are bickering over"). Finally, Newsted said: "James is on quite a few records: in the South Park movie, when Kenney goes to hell, James is singing, and he's on just about every Corrosion Of Conformity album. That's a shot at him, but I'm going to keep it. I can't play my shit, but he can go play with other people".

Reminiscences of older, more innocent times were entertaining, with Kirk claiming: "We would drink day in and day out and hardly come up for air. People would be dropping

like flies all around us, but we had the tolerance built up. Our reputation started to precede us. I can't remember the Kill 'Em All tour – we used to start drinking at three or four in the afternoon". However, he also mused: "I was abused as a child. My dad drank a lot. He beat the shit out of me and my mom quite a bit. I got ahold of a guitar, and from the time I was 15, I rarely left my room. I remember having to pull my dad off my mom when he attacked her one time, during my 16th birthday – he turned on me and started slapping me around. Then my dad just left one day. My mom was struggling to support me and my sister. I've definitely channeled a lot of anger into the music. I was also abused by my neighbour when I was like nine or 10. The guy was a sick fuck. He had sex with my dog, Tippy. I can laugh about it now – hell, I was laughing about it then".

Booze soon raised its ugly head: James said, "I had to have a bottle of vodka just for fun. I'm surprised I'm still alive", and Jason remarked, "James is the only one that ever drank so much he couldn't show up for a rehearsal or for photos. He is the only one who ever actually poisoned himself". James added: "Around the time of Load, I felt I wanted to stop drinking. 'Maybe I'm missing out on something. Everyone else seems so happy all the time. I want to get happy.' I'd plan my life around a hangover: 'The Misfits are playing in town Friday night, so Saturday is hangover day.' I lost a lot of days in my life. Going to therapy for a year, I learned a lot about myself. There's a lot of things that scar you when you're growing up, you don't know why. The song 'Bleeding Me' is about that: I was trying to bleed out all bad, get the evil out. While I was going through therapy, I discovered some ugly stuff in there. A dark spot... I took more than a year off from drinking – and the skies didn't part. It was just life, but less fun. The evil didn't come out. I wasn't laughing, wasn't having a good time. I realised, drinking is a part of me. Now I know how far to go... I wouldn't say I'm an alcoholic – but then, you know, alcoholics say they're not alcoholics".

On the subject of drugs, Kirk recalled: "Cocaine has definitely been in our lives. You hang out with other musicians, and next thing you know, you have five guys crammed into a bathroom stall. I had a bad coke problem on the ...And Justice For All tour, but I pulled out of that, because it makes me depressed, basically. I tried smack once. I was so thankful that I hated it". Lars added: "I tried acid once; I was shit-fucking scared. The only drug I've ever really engaged in is cocaine. It gave me another couple of hours of drinking. A lot of people use it as a way to get closer to you, and you fall for that. I go through cycles where I say, OK, I'm going to pull away for a while. And then I take six months away".

All this negativity seemed to infect the band's professional activities, with half-completed recording sessions started and abandoned here and there. In between attempting to lay down tracks with Bob Rock deputising on bass, Lars took a break to become a father for the second time and do a NWOBHM radio show on the KSJO station, James went bear-hunting in Russia (missing his son's first birthday in the process) and Kirk jammed with Vitamin T at Sammy Hagar's Cabo Wabo Cantina club, on a cover of 'Until It Sleeps', as well as doing a lot of surfing.

In July Napster formally accepted the settlement of their dispute, with Lars stating: "I think we've resolved this in a way that works for fans, recording artists and songwriters alike, Our beef hasn't been with the concept of sharing music; everyone knows that we've never objected to our fans trading tapes of our live concert performances. The problem we had with Napster was that they never asked us or other artists if we wanted to participate in their business. We believe that this settlement will create the kind of enhanced protection for artists that we've been seeking from Napster. We await Napster's implementation of a new model which will allow artists to choose how their creative efforts are distributed. It's good that they're going legit."

And then it happened: on 19 July Metallica announced, "James Hetfield has entered a rehabilitation facility to undergo treatment for alcoholism and other addictions… [he] has entered an undisclosed facility, and he will continue to receive treatment until further notice. Until then, we have postponed all current activities, including recording sessions for our new album."

No-one was surprised, and most were sympathetic. James had always been the most introverted member of Metallica and the first to require a drink to lubricate his on-stage persona. Of course, rumours began to spread: the 'other addictions' part of the statement had people wondering if Hetfield had problems with drugs, too. However, Jason Newsted explained to the press: "I think that one thing that really needs to be cleared up, that I'm not sure how it's been misconstrued, is that the other addictions have nothing to do with substances. As long as I have known him, he has never touched anything other than alcohol. I know for a fact that he's never done any kind of amphetamines, cocaine or anything like that in his life ever. I know he's never done LSD or ecstasy or any of that shit ever. Any of that thing that people think has to do with drugs is completely wrong… It had to do with the breaking up of the band, too, and some other personal things. Emotionally, he maybe was really drunk with, I don't know, with sadness, tense things or stress. It kinda caught up with him all at once. But he's not a weak person, as you well know. He's a very strong person. It's just what had to happen for him to keep himself together and for him to be able to go on".

With this, Metallica fell silent. The fanbase waited for what would happen next…

The next year brought plenty of exposure for Metallica, but no real news about Hetfield's progress or the status of the band,

other than a general sense that things were in stasis. Kirk and Lars, holding the fort at Metallica HQ (a working place that the band had fitted out for themselves in recent times) with the ever-present Bob Rock, performed the occasional engagement – such as a truly poor rap-metal track with producer Swizz Beatz and rapper Ja Rule – but didn't do much else of note. It later emerged that the band had hired a film crew headed up by documentary-makers Joe Berlinger and Bruce Sinofsky to make a promotional clip about the making of the next album, some months before James entered rehab. This crew was now reduced to hanging around HQ, archiving the events without really knowing what would happen to their project.

Rumours continued to abound, with one entertaining idea that Dave Ellefson of the recently folded Megadeth (Dave Mustaine had injured his arm and dissolved the line-up) would join Metallica for the bass slot. Then Lars auctioned off his collection of fine art, including a set of Basquiat works, netting five million dollars in the process, as well as selling his house for more than twice that figure.

When James emerged, sober and smiling, from rehab, Lars and Kirk welcomed him back with open arms. Musical activity was tentative to begin with, although the band did record some songs for a Ramones tribute album, play a surprise show at the Kimo's club with Bob Rock on bass and contribute a Waylon Jennings song to another tribute album (this last was James' own work – he sang and played guitar, bass and drums). The rest of 2002 was taken up with recording sessions and fun events such as the fanclub party at HQ (at which two fans jammed with the band) and giving away a day with the band as a charity prize (it fetched $23,000 on eBay).

Of the revelations that had come to him in rehab, James explained: "I've been in Metallica since I was 19 years old, which can be a very unusual environment, and it's very easy to find yourself not knowing how to live outside of that environment, which is what happened to me. I didn't know anything about life. I didn't know that I could come home and live a family life. I didn't know that I could live my life in a different way to how it was in the band since I was 19, which was very excessive and very intense. And if you have addictive behaviour then you can't always make the best choices for yourself. And I definitely didn't make the best choices for myself.

"But rehab is like college for your head. I really learned some things about myself in there. I was able to reframe my life and not look at everything with a negative connotation. That's how I was raised. It was like a survival technique for me. And getting into Metallica meant that initially I had to fight to survive, for food, for the towel, for the shower, for everything. And then fighting to be the best band you can be, and putting other bands down. Finding fault with everything was how Metallica was fuelled. And not only did I play a part in that, I was buried in that."

Hetfield was finding it difficult to be James the man rather than James the star: "I felt that I couldn't show any weakness. For me, I was James Hetfield of Metallica rather than just James Hetfield. And I was trying to live that lifestyle at home; I was trying to wear that mask all the time. And it's amazing how long you can wear a mask for. We're performers who play music, I mean, this is us. This isn't an act. But now I've learned how to be more congruent with where I am. Admitting that sometimes being on tour really sucks, and that I would rather go home. Or that I'm not in a good mood right now, and not worrying if people turn round and say hey, you're an asshole. That can't hurt me now, whereas I used to be so concerned that people liked me. There's a lot of machismo in this world, but I suppose the most manly thing you can do is face up to your weaknesses and expose them. And you're showing strength by exposing your weaknesses to people. And that opens up a dialogue, it opens up friendships, which is definitely what it has done for me".

Lars admitted that at one point he had wondered if the band was over: "I wanted to go and visit him; I wanted to make things better. But I couldn't. And all the time your imagination is running away with itself when you don't have any real info – we didn't hear from James for months. Your mind starts to think of the worst that can happen, and I honestly wondered if this was the end for Metallica... I thought, you know, we'd had a good run but that this might be it". As for Kirk, he recalled that James had been at a surprise birthday party held for him in November 2001: "Seeing him was one of the greatest birthday [presents] I ever had. It was just so great to see him again. I'm even getting emotional talking about it now".

However, hackles were raised among old-school Metallica fans yet again when the band announced that a 2003 tour with Limp Bizkit, Linkin Park and Deftones would take place. The choice of openers was odd: while Deftones were peaking, the heyday of both Limp Bizkit and Linkin Park had definitely passed, with both bands gaining most commercial success in 2000 but fading away as the nu-metal movement died. Jason Newsted, who had by now joined thrash metallers Voivod and launched the Chophouse label, was disgusted, telling Classic Rock: "I can't even get my breath about that. I'm absolutely flabbergasted... As a fan of theirs I'm very disappointed and freaked out by all this. They had the opportunity to come back as leaders, to take out bands such as In Flames, Strapping Young Lad and Voivod – bands that deserve to be seen. Metallica are the only ones with that kind of opportunity. Do they really think it'll sell them more than a couple of fucking thousand tickets if Linkin Park – or whoever – are on that bill? No, there are people out there who still want metal, and it's too bad it wasn't addressed in that way".

Auditions for a select set of bass players took place in December: candidates' identities were kept secret at the time, but it was later revealed that among them were Scott Reeder of Kyuss/Unida, Danny Lohner of Nine Inch Nails, Jane's Addiction's Eric Avery, sometime Marilyn Manson player Twiggy Ramirez and Ozzy Osbourne/Suicidal Tendencies/ Infectious Grooves/Black Label Society's Robert Trujillo. In February 2003 it was announced that Trujillo, a phenomenal player, had been asked to join – and excitement was felt throughout the Metallica camp.

Lars was beside himself: "When Rob came to San Francisco the first time and jammed with us, we all felt this incredible magic between the four of us. It was just something that we could not describe, we all just knew it. Bob Rock told us right after the jam, that it sounded like a fucking 747 taking off! I am so fucking excited to be a full unit again... The last two years of just being the three of us have taught me so much about myself, about James and Kirk and about Metallica. And to welcome Rob into Metallica in 2003 after all the growth and soul-searching we've been through for the last two years,

feels so fucking awesome. Being at full strength again is at this moment indescribable".

Kirk added, "Rob's chemistry with the band is undeniable. From the first rehearsal Rob was just mind-blowing, because he had such a huge sound and he pulled with his fingers, which is very reminiscent of Cliff Burton and we really liked that sound. He delivered on all fronts. He had a big sound and on top of that he's really a great, solid guy". As for James: "He pounds. The power that comes through his fingers. He's a ball of energy and he's so calm and able and balanced. He's got great stuff to offer but his personality is just right. He's on fire, he's ready, he's plugged right into the strength of Metallica and helping it shine".

Trujillo's first outing with the band came when MTV recorded an MTV Icon show in their honour: the band played a set after a group of other acts performed Metallica songs – Korn, Staind, Avril Lavigne, Limp Bizkit, Sum 41 and (bizarrely) Snoop Dogg among them. This came amid news that a new Metallica album, with the initially rather curious title of St. Anger, would be released in June. Fans hoped that it would feature a heavier direction than the terminally lame Loads, but most were resigned to another weak album – until, that is, postings from the band began to appear at Metallica.com comparing the new music to death metallers Entombed and hardcore scene-leaders Hatebreed. Could St. Anger be the way back to metal credibility for Metallica?

When the record appeared, it debuted at No. 1 in the US, boosted by a value-added package including a bonus live DVD in which the band ran through the album in the studio. As the track-by-track analysis below confirms, the album was a complete shock for most people – some of the fast riffing and aggression of old was back, but the sound of the album was truly, truly terrible. Lars had loosened the snares on the snare drum, leading critics to mention 'garbage can' drums, and

Bob Rock went on the record defending its unusual sound. He said: "It's almost like forming a band again, you know, that's really what has happened here in my opinion, is forming a band again... Getting together and laying a whole pile of ideas down, and just watching as you listen to the ideas that you did last week, you go somewhere else or you feel like you have to go somewhere else. During the Load and Reload period there was a part where James was looking at twenty-eight-plus songs that he had to write lyrics for. It was a daunting task and it was just too much for him, you know, to look at all of those songs. That's one of the reasons why it turned into two albums, but still it was just, he was just staring at these blank pages of music that he had to write lyrics to. And so what we did right away... as soon as we started making music was get the ball rolling right away".

Rock added: "It feels... like a really old tough English boxer who is hard as nails and drinks whiskey and is going against a young guy that is really, really strong and really agile and stuff, but the old guy beats the absolute shit out of him. These are middle-aged guys that have a wealth of experience, that have a wealth of taste and ability, just really beating the shit out of their emotions in music and I love it... I think that this stuff is going to make a really big statement, that's what I would say".

Lars told the writer Martin Popoff of Brave Words & Bloody Knuckles that "I think we were sort of guilty in the past, especially the Load and Reload stuff, of not editing ourselves. So we're dealing with that at the moment, which is kind of weird... We're trying not to beat the life out of it, which I think we had done on the previous couple of records. It got to the point where we produced all the life out of it. So there's some really great moments, some energy, some moments of people playing music together in a room, and it has a lot of soul".

However, the album sounded horrible, and the songs were poor too – there was far too much mid-tempo riffing and

the vocals were out of tune. Furthermore, Kirk had not been permitted to record one single solo. Fans were aghast, and still are, three years later.

Metallica, riding an enormous wave of public debate between those who were horrified and those who were defensive, took to the road as promised and executed an enormous, $60 million-grossing tour, broken sporadically for rest breaks. Four singles – 'Frantic', 'St. Anger' 'Some Kind Of Monster' and 'The Unnamed Feeling' – kept their profile high: in Finland, for example, no fewer than six Metallica albums re-entered the Top 40. A missed slot at the UK's Download festival in June 2004 by Lars was cause for concern: "We'd had a heavy touring schedule, we'd been in Japan and Europe and America and Australia", he told Metal Hammer. "In the midst of all that there were things that had come unravelled in my personal life – my family and my marriage and stuff – and all of that happened right at the time when we were going through some pretty demanding tour stuff. I'd had a lot of late nights and early mornings with cousins and whatever. So I woke up in Copenhagen on the Sunday morning, I had brunch with 14 in-laws and cousins and then I went straight out to the airport. I got on the plane, and I was so exhausted."

He continued: "We took off, it was just me and my friend Steve, and about halfway over to Midlands Airport... I don't know what the fuck happened, but all of a sudden I just fuckin' lost it, and I had never quite experienced anything like that before. It was pretty fuckin' scary to be in a little fuckin' metal tube at 41,000 feet... I've never had anxiety attacks or any kind of stress attacks ever. It was fuckin' freaky, dude. So I'm sitting there sucking on an oxygen mask and I'm like, fuck this, I need to get this checked out, so we landed in Hamburg and went to the hospital.

"They took some blood tests and everything was completely normal physically," he said, "it was just everything caught up with me mentally. At about six o'clock I was talking to James and Kirk and Peter Mensch from my hospital bed, and I was saying, I'm gonna get on a plane. And they were like, listen, you're not getting on any fuckin' plane – stay the fuck in bed and chill out for a couple of days and we'll manage without you. I was saying, dude, I'm not gonna lay here in Hamburg while you guys are playing the coolest gig in the entire metal universe! But we all agreed that it was the right thing, and by this time James and Kirk told me that they'd talked with some of the other bands and they were gonna pull it off."

Ruefully, Ulrich laughs: "It was the first Metallica gig I'd missed, ever – I was the only one left with a perfect track record! I swear to you, I was lying there with an IV in me and there was a window at the other end of the room – and I was like, fuck this, I'm gonna pull the IV out, jump through the window and make a run for it! Anyway, it was weird, but a couple of things came out of it. For the first time I realised what James had gone through in all the times when he had missed gigs and watched Kid Rock and Jonathan Davis step up. And it made me realise that – and I don't want this to be misinterpreted – but it's still just a rock'n'roll show."

Lar's place on the Metallica drum stool was taken by Slayer's Dave Lombardo and Slipknot's Joey Jordison – a sobering experience for him. As he remarked, "You try laying in a hospital in Germany while Dave Lombardo – the greatest drummer on the planet – is playing with your band! That's not easy. Joey Jordison, too. It was a pretty fucked-up day. I'm kinda like, that didn't really happen, did it? After a few days of sleep, I was thinking, did I dream that? I was disheartened to think that people would have travelled from all over England and beyond to come to this show, and then we didn't step up – but at the same time, it made me realise how proud I am of the fact that we always do the best we can and we always go the extra mile, and that sometimes you gotta do what the fuck you've gotta do. And there was life on the other side of that – people were respectful. I have a bit of an odd relationship with it – I still haven't really looked at any of the press for it, or the pictures… I fuckin' hope it would be a great show. If seeing Dave Lombardo and Joey Jordison playing with Metallica isn't a great show, then I don't know what is! I wish I could have seen it too, although the whole thing is such a mindfuck. I feel bad for the kids who made the trip, but at the same time I know they got to see something truly unique."

In July the long-promised Berlinger & Sinofsky Metallica film, Some Kind Of Monster, was released to cinemas and caused an immediate sensation. A three-hour edit of over 1600 hours shot over the two-to-three-year period that the team were following Metallica's every move, the movie traced the band's development – professionally and personally – from the end of the Napster issue and Jason's departure to the live debut of tracks from St. Anger. The core of the narrative is the group therapy sessions that the band-members underwent, accompanied by a 'performance coach' called Phil Towle. Towle – who had been recruited to attempt to keep Jason in the band and stayed on afterwards – was chosen for his track record with sports stars and bands such as Rage Against The Machine, with whom he had attempted to solve interpersonal issues. As it happens, the film doesn't portray him in the best light: bizarrely, although he obviously assists the band, particularly Lars and James, through the mutual problems they face, the scene where they fire him on camera is both shocking and revealing.

High points are many, especially on the DVD version which added another seven hours of extra footage. Lars is seen sipping champagne at the fine art auction which netted him five million bucks, watching the action from a private viewing room while orchestral Metallica songs play in the background – a fantastic piece of rock-star tomfoolery. James talks with evident difficulty about his childhood, piloting a variety of souped-up sports cars, and slams the door on a therapy meeting on his way to rehab. Kirk takes the camera around his house, a kind of Addams Family mansion full of gothic artwork, animal skulls and oppressive wood panelling, before attending a driving school as a penalty for speeding. Jason spits that the recruitment of Towle was "so fucking lame" and his new band, Echobrain, give Lars temporary paranoia that Metallica are the past and Jason's new act is the future. Rob's awe-inspiring audition – he chooses to play 'Battery' at ferocious speed – is shown in full, as are the performances by the other candidates. Notably, they're all nervous and sweating while trying to to match up to James' fearsome riffing, while Trujillo slides effortlessly into the role. When Lars offers him a million dollars to join the band, recoupable against tour earnings, he is visibly stunned.

A key scene in which Lars faces up to none other than Dave Mustaine in an effort to dispel mutual demons is cringe-making but totally watchable, with the Megadeth frontman bitter, tearful

and pale. He says to Lars with understandable venom, "Do you have any idea what it was like for me?", to which the drummer has no real answer. Dave later complained that the scene had been included in the movie against his wishes, to which director Berlinger later explained that Mustaine had signed a consent form and had little reason for complaint, as he had not actually yet seen the film in its full form.

Some Kind Of Monster cost the band – according to Berlinger's 2004 book, Metallica: This Monster Lives – in the region of seven million dollars to create, a microscopic total compared to the average Hollywood blockbuster thanks to the cheap digital video technology. It took 'only' two million dollars at the box office, although it would have recouped some more from the DVD release – but this issue didn't bother Metallica, who had released it as a personal message to their fans. James later said that he had initially regarded Some Kind Of Monster as the accompanying documentary to the St. Anger album, but in the wake of his rehab, the band therapy and what was effectively a type of rebirth, he amended this, observing rather that the album was merely the soundtrack to the real creative triumph – the movie. As so many fans were disillusioned by the poor quality of St. Anger, it's easy to agree.

2005 was a quiet year for Metallica, with new studio sessions underway at last and a palpable sense of relief among fans that Trujillo's presence might spur the band back into aggressive mode. Some dates supporting the Rolling Stones were indicators of Metallica's enormous stature, and Kirk worked on guitar for Carlos Santana's new album. Otherwise, the world is waiting with baited breath...

We will see what the next couple of years bring: if Metallica, now in their mid-40s, do call it a day soon – as is also popularly rumoured – then at least we will have their unique back catalogue to enjoy.

UP CLOSE AND PERSONAL

METALLICA TURNED the American metal scene upside down when they arrived with their debut album, Kill 'Em All, released in June 1983. Taking their cues from the New Wave of British Heavy Metal, singer-rhythm guitarist James Hetfield, drummer Lars Ulrich, lead guitarist Kirk Hammett (who had replaced Dave Mustaine, who would go on to play an important part in the scene himself with his band Megadeth), and bassist Cliff Burton delivered 40 minutes of non-stop thrash metal, excepting Burton's brilliant bass solo, 'Pulling Teeth'.

The band's albums became increasingly ambitious, culminating in 1986's Master of Puppets, a recognized classic. Metallica hit a commercial peak in 1991 with their eponymous fifth album, known as the black album among fans. This stripped-down effort spawned the MTV favourites 'Enter Sandman' and 'Nothing Else Matters', and proved divisive among the band's hardcore followers. An extensive three-year stadium tour followed, confirming Metallica's status as international metal superstars.

These interviews offer an insight into the unique phenomenon that is Metallica through interviews with their personal photographer and friend Harold O, journalist Joel McIver, and, to begin with, Martin Hooker, the founder of important British indie label Music For Nations.

Music For Nations was Metallica's home in the UK and Europe for their first three albums. The records that the band cut with Hooker and his label are considered by many hardcore fans to be their best work. After all, Metallica first got a foothold in Europe, and it was this success that convinced a major label to get involved with them. In short, if it wasn't for Hooker and his company, the history of modern rock may have been radically different.

At the time Metallica were signed, who was on your label? What kind of label was it?

MH: Well, it was very, very early days for Music For Nations. I'd previously had a label called Secret, which was a punk-only label that had been incredibly successful. We'd had nine releases, and all nine went Top 40. It was all very exciting. I had left a major to start that label, so I thought, "This is a piece of piss! Just release a record it goes in the chart – easy." Naïve, but that was the way it happened. We sold the company to Virgin. The last band I signed to Secret was Twisted Sister, so I was moving away from the punk thing and into glam-metal, really. I thought, "Heavy metal is the one thing that you can sell in every country in the world. It's never in fashion, so it never goes out of fashion. Once you get people hooked on an artist they will stay with them forever." So we started Music for Nations. It was world-wide music.

We signed a couple of bands: Virgin Steele, who are still strutting their stuff around Europe, and Metallica, who were only the second band that we signed. We certainly got off to a good start. Their manager at the time, Johnny Z, sent me a tape. The front cover showed a very unpleasant sword coming out of a toilet; it was called Metal Up Your Ass.

I listened to it and thought, "Wow! Crap! This is fantastic!" I know it seems weird to say it now, but at that time no one had heard of speed or thrash or whatever, so it was a completely new phenomenon. I played it to a few people and they actually thought I was having a laugh. A couple of my friends at EMI were rolling around on the floor – but I had strength in my convictions; I really thought that we could do something with it.

Push came to shove, I did the deal with Johnny Z, and we

had them in the UK and in Europe, and Johnny had them on his label Megaforce in America. Metal Up Your Ass became Kill 'Em All, which was an interesting album. It broke a lot of moulds and set new standards for a lot of groups. We were not sure what was going to happen when we put it out. I was really excited, but I can remember we did an initial pressing of 3,000 for the whole of Europe, and we didn't sell half of them in the first month. I was thinking, "Oh, I really stuffed this one," but we kept plugging on and plugging on. Just recently, I looked back through the old manufacturing records that we had at the time, and we were redoing them 500 at a time. If we had only known that in 18 months time it was going to be a gold record, I could have saved myself an awful lot of money!

We had some other bands at the time, like The Rods and Exciter, and we decided that the way to go would be to put tours together – bring all these American bands over and put them out together. We were already doing quite well with The Rods, because they were established. Exciter were doing quite well, and Metallica were the new kids on the block. The whole tour got cancelled because of lack of interest. We didn't sell any tickets for that tour, but within a year Metallica would be playing enormous venues. We ended up spending over £100,000 on tour support in the first year, putting them out with Motörhead and all sorts, anybody that we thought that was right.

I remember bringing them over once; I think we did the old Marquee club [in London]. My god, I mean, you have never seen anything like it. It was fantastic. Never has so much hair been flung in violence. It was great. Once the word of mouth started, it just snowballed and snowballed and snowballed. In the end we would be inundated with interview requests and this and that. I still think it's funny that their very first front cover was the NME, and very few people know that.

That was the strange thing. Everyone was like, "What

the hell is thrash all about?" Then there was this big picture of James [Hetfield] with his hair everywhere, and we had it pinned up on the wall in the office. It was a great picture, and after that everybody wanted them on their front cover. To think that the NME had something to do with their success is quite strange.

They started to get bigger and bigger, and then we did Ride the Lightning. It was a completely different situation for them. By that time, Johnny Z had run out of money, so we stepped in and said, "All right, we will pay to record it," because obviously I believed in them. We set them up in Denmark in this little studio with Flemming Rasmussen. A few weeks went by. So, I'm on the phone to Lars [Ulrich], and nobody speaks more than Lars, bless his heart. He kept saying, "No, no, no – everything is great, man. Everything is on course. It's fantastic."

Another couple of weeks went by, and I'm thinking that they must be getting on for the finish now. When they told me that they didn't have any rough tracks to send me, I got on a plane to Denmark! The first thing I discovered was that there was an Elephant beer dispenser in the reception, so my suspicions were aroused immediately.

When I went in, they were still working on the drum sound, six weeks in! We ended up kicking some arse and having some conversations, and in the end they got on with it. In the meantime, a deal had been done with Elektra Records in North America, and by the time Ride the Lightning was finished it was actually a stunning record, a really stunning record.

It was a turning point for them, and a benchmark for lots of other bands. We came away from the studio with a record that we were all really proud of, and that I was prepared to go balls-to-the-wall to promote. It instantly took off, and dragged Kill 'Em All with it – it was astonishing. It snowballed and snowballed. They were doing these big tours on their own, playing stadiums in parts of Europe. We suddenly got the feeling that this band could be a world phenomenon.

Elektra loved the album, and it did so well that they agreed to pay for the next one. So we got Master of Puppets for free, and that was the one that kicked it all off big-time, because that was, and I think still is, their best album, but to get that for free was incredible for us, and it helped me turn the company around. We had already got bands like Megadeth, W.A.S.P. and Manowar, so we were on a roll as well. It was good.

The band had everything; they had a great front man who knew how to kick arse and really convey that aggression. He could be intimidating when he wanted to be, and powerful when he wanted to be, but in interviews he was incredibly shy and didn't want to know. For that sort of thing, they could take the man on the drums, bring him forward, and you have got the gift that all groups and record companies want. With Lars, you can't stop the guy talking. He is articulate, incredibly intelligent, and one of the best people I have ever worked with. He is a record company's dream, because you could just stick him in front of any journalist, and that journalist is going to have more material in half an hour than he is going to get from a dozen bands in a fortnight. Lars really played his part, and each one of them had their own role and their own image. They were very, very on the case. Then, obviously, we had the road accident where we lost the bass player [Cliff Burton], which was tragic, and for a while they were going to split up. It was just awful. Luckily, things changed.

They decided to bring in a new manager. We had discussions about me managing them, among other things, and then Pete Mensch came on the scene. He decided to take the band over, and signed them to Polygram, because he already had Def Leppard there, so for him it was 'better the devil you know' than a small independent label, albeit one that were doing a fantastic job.

So he signed the band to Polygram, and the next album [...
And Justice For All] was a raging stiff. They had had three gold
albums in the UK to kick off with, but nobody at Polygram
had ever heard of the band and it was kind of embarrassing.
The album just barely scraped silver, after quite some time. The
band came over to do a tour, and we were presenting them with
platinum discs and whatever while they kept all the Polygram
people standing outside, in the corridor. So that was a funny
moment. The band were always going to be enormous, because
it was something completely new, and something that a lot of
kids at that time could really relate to: the frenzy, the energy! I
mean, you saw them on stage in the early days – they were raw
and nasty, but, hell, that was great.

**What was the difference in how you promoted them and how
Polygram promoted them? It does seem strange that when
they were riding such a wave of success, what with Master
of Puppets and the back catalogue, and then nothing. It just
drops off with ... And Justice For All. Is it to do with the way
the record company promoted them, do you think?**
MH: To us, they were the most important thing on the planet.
Everything that my whole team were doing 24/7 was for
Metallica, even though what was good for Metallica was good
for our other groups; we had big hit albums with Megadeth and
all those sort of people on the strength of it. We ended up having
56 different acts in the chart in a fairly short space of time, which
not many labels can say these days – certainly not indie labels.

So what we learnt with them, we used over and over again.
We just treated them like they were the most important thing
on the label, and of course when they went to Polygram, half
of the people had never heard of them. They must've been like,
"Well, we don't want to hang out with a bunch of greasy, long-
haired guys whose music we hate." They wanted to hang out
with whoever was the latest trend on Polygram at that time.

There was no sympathetic feeling there, and I think that had a lot to do with it.

Metallica just didn't realise it at the time, because they were being shoehorned into the deal by the management. I may be doing [Polygram] an injustice, but that was what it looked like to us at the time, that they just didn't understand what a hot property they had got. Not to realise how hot a band is when they have already had three gold albums is a bit naïve. It was one of those things. It was a shame. Eventually, they woke up, their light bulb went off, and they got behind it. It took a long time for them to wake up; it really did.

Who was dealing with them around the time of Cliff's death? Was it you who spoke to them? I just wonder really. You always wonder who is supporting the bands when things go wrong. Did their management fulfil that role, or did you?
MH: I would like to say we took that role, but we didn't really. We all spoke to them, and I'm sure that Johnny Z spoke to them as well, because he was probably still as close to them as anybody. I know I spoke to them, but [whether or not to carry on] was very much a decision that they had to come to by themselves. They took some time off to decide what they were going to do, and, you know, I am very pleased that they made the right decision, and I'm sure they are as well. I always had the feeling that it was touch and go, and that it could have gone either way. These things happen. I mean, these things happen to a lot of groups. Sometimes it can be something much more minor that goes wrong, and the band falls apart – but this band was stronger than that. They had that self-belief. I think that Lars probably had more to do with it than anybody; he had that strength to hold things together. Once again, I wasn't party to what was going on, but knowing the band as I do, I can imagine a lot of the strength coming from Lars. He is a very strong character.

Why was it easy for them to be released from the record deal with you guys? Were they just bought out?

MH: It was one of those situations where we originally did a deal with their management for a three-album deal. They had fulfilled their part of it. We could have gone back in after the third album, renegotiated and done a couple more albums. There was talk about that when I was in the frame for managing the band, but Mensch came in and wanted to take it somewhere else. Obviously, I was gutted to lose the band, but we were satisfied that we had helped create an enormous band. We also had Twisted Sister selling X-million of every album that they were doing, so I had broken two stadium bands, which was fantastic.

Why do you think that the trilogy Metallica released on your label is perceived as the golden era? How much of that is down to band line-up, how much of it is down to the way that you guys promoted it, and how much is down to circumstances?

MH: Well, you're not going to have a great record without a great line-up. It is just not really possible. They were also doing something that was very, very new. Nobody else was doing it at that time, although a million bands came out of the Bay area after that, or the Bay area of Hull or the Bay area of... Everybody soon cottoned on to it. A little bit like they did with the punk thing. Shit, I could do that.

Still, they were the masters of it, and they were fantastic at it. They were very, very tight. I mean, you can listen to a lot of bands that are still doing that type of music, even though Metallica have moved on dramatically. I mean, I still get a hundred demos a day from bands doing Kill 'Em All. It's like, "Wake up! This was 1983, and the world's moved on now," but at the time, it was a brand-new sound. They were incredibly good at it, and they signed to a label that totally, totally believed in them and had the finance to do whatever they needed to do within a European situation.

We didn't have the clout to do it in America, but then they managed to do that themselves through Elektra, so that was great. With those first three albums, each one got better and better, and I think one of my proudest moments ever with that band was the launch day for Master of Puppets. There was a big heavy-metal record shop at the time called Shades, and they were based in Soho. This one record shop took so much stock of that record that you wouldn't believe it. They filled the shop, and they had them already bagged with the till receipt, in piles next to the counter – just piles everywhere.

The queue came out of the shop, because the punters were queuing before the shop was open, and it snaked all the way through Soho. These kids were all coming in for the one record. I mean, I was standing outside that shop, and I had tears in my eyes. It meant that everything I had done was totally justified, because the kids absolutely loved this band, and they paid the kids back in spades, because here we are twenty-plus years later, and they are still going strong, still selling out stadiums. Despite all their on-off problems, which nobody needs to drag out, they are still here, and they are still as big as they ever were.

What did they think of Britain? Were they very much at home here because of the fans?
MH: I mean, I can't speak for them. Certainly they always had a really big buzz here, and they actually had an awful lot more success here and in Europe than they did in America. It took a long time for the Americans to wake up to the fact that they had bred a great band, as it did with Twisted Sister and all those other bands. They all had chart albums in the UK before they had ever done anything in America. They weren't here on that particular occasion, but when they heard about it, I think that

they were kind of amused. There were police controlling the crowds, etc. It was quite funny.

You talked about the protracted recording schedule for Ride the Lightning. How long did Master of Puppets take to record? It's such an amazing album, and the sound is pretty spot on, isn't it?

MH: I have to say, in all honesty, I have no recollection whatsoever how long that took. That's all in the addled part of my mind that's long since ceased to function. I think that it was much more controlled. They had producers and budgets and people in America overseeing them all the time [because it was paid for by Elektra]. At that time they were also a tighter working unit, and they had had plenty of time on the road to write the songs. Unfortunately, a lot of groups will come up with their first album in what seems like a very short amount of time, but that first album has probably taken them two years to write. Then you put them out on the road for six months, and then back in the studio, and you expect another album in the next couple of months, and of course nine times out of ten they have done bugger all. But Metallica were always fairly strong in that respect. They were always writing and always working on new material, so they didn't usually find the same problems, I don't think.

Who decided how to book all the tours? I mean they just endlessly toured under you guys ...

MH: They did. We toured them non-stop because I felt that it was the only way, since we weren't going to get any radio play. We weren't going to get any mainstream press. I mean, courtesy of Kerrang! and a couple of other magazines at the time, like Metal Hammer, we did have some kind of small media presence, but you needed to get them out there and show people just how great this band really was.

It was also much easier to pull a crowd for an American band than it is for an English band. You can't blame the kids for that; there is something a little bit more exotic about a band from Los Angeles than a band from Cleethorpes. There is always the chance that they might not get to see this band again. Wherever they played they just brought the house down, and in some cases a little bit more of the house than we wanted – plasterwork falling of the walls – but they were a great band live, and if you've got a great live band, you have play to your strengths. We pumped more and more money in, but we got it back 10 times over. These days, trust me, it's a lot harder. You can pump a fortune into a live show and never see a fraction of it back. It's changed a lot. TV advertising seems to rule the day.

Who dealt with their image – things like album covers and that side of things? Was that all just very ad hoc and whatever the band wanted?
MH: To an extent, wherever possible, I like to leave that to the group. I mean, that band didn't really have an image, and that was one of things that they liked. I mean, you look at Cliff and you look at James, and they seemed to be from different bands. It was an anti-image almost. They didn't give a shit, and that worked as well.

I thought that the Kill 'Em All cover was great. I think that Lars came up with a lot of the ideas, he ran them all by the group, and they would make the final decision between them. Most of the ideas would come from the band, and if you've got a band with strong ideas, you should let them go with it, because, after all, who knows their market better than the band themselves? They know the kids that they are trying to appeal to, and they know what those kids like, because they are the same age as those kids. I mean, they were so young. When you look at the picture on the back of Kill 'Em All..., I mean, you have never seen so many spots between four people. They were

89

just kids, but they were appealing to kids of that age. "I'm a spotty little Herbert; I could be doing that." That's fantastic. They knew who they were appealing to, so I let them get on with it.

It's interesting that you mention that. How did they change over the years when they were with you? Did they change very much? Did they have the same dreams and aspirations?

MH: I guess so. I think that their dreams changed somewhat, because I don't think that they ever in a million years dreamt that they would be as all-encompassingly enormous as they became. You know, it's like being a footballer and suddenly realizing that you are going to be Pele. It just doesn't happen. They were very lucky that their dreams did come true. In the same way that – not every band can become Coldplay, or whoever the flavour of the month is. They just wanted to be as good as they could be. They went from very simple stage shows, where it was just a sea of hair spinning round and round, to these enormous things with mosh pits and whatever. It was just fantastic. It's a band progressing, using their intelligence, taking ideas on board – both internally from the band and from other people – learning, and growing. There has to be organic growth. Otherwise it's going to stagnate.

Did you ever get to watch the gigs very much? Did you get to go out on the road with them? How difficult was it?

MH: I went on the road with them quite a lot in the early years, and they were a lot of fun. A lot of fun. I think that the most fun for me was to see the size of the venues increasing, the size of the crowds increasing, and the number of nights they played at a single venue increasing from the beginning of a tour to the end. Everything was changing, and that's probably the biggest buzz you can ever have in this industry, because you know that the band is doing something right, you are doing something right, and everything is kicking off. You don't get that very often.

You are really seeing something happen before your eyes?
MH: Yeah, yeah.

Who was your tour booker? Did you always have one person?
MH: We always had a say in what was going on. A lot of the times people would phone up and say, "Hey, listen, we have this band going out; we want a special guest." If you have a band that is suddenly the hot band at the time, you can get them on with a bigger band in bigger venues, because your band is going to help sell that venue out and put bums on seats. It still happens now. You get really huge bands actually turning up as special guests to somebody a bit bigger, and you think, "What the hell is that all about?" – but they are probably being paid very nicely for it, because they make sure that the gig is a sell-out. We used to do that wherever possible, and we started to get them on festivals and things like that. Once you get them on at the festivals, then it kind of self-propels itself. Suddenly, 70,000 people are seeing them all at once, and it takes on a life of its own.

The band refused to do music videos for a long time. Was it ever an option? Was it discussed?
MH: It was discussed, and it was thrown out. It was re-discussed, and it was thrown out again. I didn't care to be honest. I thought that because music video was suddenly the thing, everybody had to do a video, but Metallica were the exception to the rule. They had all these chart records, but no music videos. I thought that was great. It just meant that the band were even more in demand live, because that was the only way the people were going to see them.

Sometimes now, the videos are overkill. Particularly in those days, there were a lot less bands making videos, and so they were shown again and again and again and again, and that's great if you are having a hit single. Metallica never chased hot singles; they were just after big album sales. I must admit, at the time I thought they were making a mistake, but I tip my hat to them now, because I think it was the right thing to do. When they did eventually do one [for 1988's 'One'], it was obviously incredibly popular.

Flemming Rasmussen. Why was he chosen? Was it somebody that Lars knew?

MH: Yeah. Once again, it is so long ago. I can only assume that, being Danish, he was someone that Lars brought in. He did a fantastic, fantastic job. I don't think he's ever really got the credit he deserves for the sound. He was working with a bunch of guys who had never done anything in a studio like that, and he brought them together brilliantly, with a great sound. You see, every year there is a Top 100 best metal albums, and all of those Metallica records figure very strongly in the Top 20, and he should get as much credibility for that as anybody. He did a great job.

Did they have a good deal with you guys? Were they lucky that they had Music for the Nations on their side? Could they have been shafted by another record company?

MH: Trust me. I always built the company up by offering a good deal to bands, because when your band is on the road, supporting two or three other bands, they all talk, and suddenly the support band, who are on your label, can say to the headlining band, "Well, actually we are on x points," and the main band are thinking, "Hang on a minute, that's three points more than we are on." You would be amazed how many headline acts we took like that. So, yeah, they had a very good deal with us, but it was good deal for them and it was a good deal for us. There is enough money to be made in the music industry for everybody to get a fair deal. There is absolutely no excuse, these days, to cut really bad deals for people. It still goes on, but there is no excuse for it.

Did they recognise their time with Music for Nations?
MH: I think so, yeah. They certainly stayed in touch, and when they are in London they always give us a call. Most bands don't. I think that is very nice. I certainly hope that they appreciate the job we did, because we did a hell of a job. To the credit of the record companies that they were with subsequently, they have done a hell of a job as well, eventually. I mean, Elektra always did a great job, and, you know, it took Polygram a while, but they did a great job subsequently.

What are your best memories of working with Metallica?
MH: Funnily enough, some of the very early shows, where they played in small venues and they were absolutely rammed. You could not shoehorn another kid in there, and the whole place was just heaving up and down. You suddenly think, "Oh, we are definitely onto something here." The one show that always stands out in my mind was when we went out to Denmark and we played this ice hockey arena. They put matting over all the ice and the band were down at one end. It was like Wembley, and it was sold out. I'm looking around and thinking, "Holy crap, who else is appearing?" – but there was no one else. We all stood on the ice, and all of the arena, all the way round, was sold out. I suddenly thought then, "Wow! If we can do this in Denmark, then this band is going all the way!"

They weren't selling when you first took them on – when they did Kill 'Em All. Was there a point when it just went click?
MH: Actually, with Kill 'Em All it was just a slow progression. You can start off with your 3,000 and it gradually trickles

through. Then you do 500 more, and then another 500. I mean, it did actually really make me laugh when we were looking through the sales-figure book that I actually kept as a memento because it was so pathetic. If you had actually known that you didn't need 3,000, you needed 350,000, it could have saved everybody a lot of time and effort.

It took a long time to sell like that, but it was doing well by the time we did Ride the Lightning. By the time Ride the Lightning came out, the reviews were stupendous. That caused an explosion in sales, and that record took off straight away. Well, I say took off. It took off to an extent. In turn, it dragged along the sales of Kill 'Em All, and then by the time we did Master of Puppets, that one actually did go through the roof from scratch. That dragged along the sales of Ride the Lightning and Kill 'Em All, so that they all went gold within weeks of each other, really. It was strange. Just to illustrate – we bought the drum kit that they recorded Ride the Lightning on, and they toured it, and it was all beaten up and rubbished, and they said, "Oh, just get rid of it, because we get endorsements now." I can remember advertising to sell that drum kit, and we didn't get one reply. If I had kept it, that would have been my pension.

Where is it?
MH: I think we sold it, in the end, for about £1,500. It's a shame, isn't it? It's just one of those odd little stories.

Do you lie awake at night thinking about that?
MH: No. Not anymore!

Why did you take on Megadeth? Was that to do with Metallica, or not at all?
MH: That was completely separate. I had never worked with [Dave] Mustaine when he was in Metallica because he was kicked out before I got my grubby little hands on them. He signed to a company called Combat Records in America, which

was owned by my partner in the UK. I licensed it. They sent me a pile of albums and I just went through them, listening to them all. They used to release tons and tons of records, and I'd just go through them, pick out the ones that I liked, and then we would release them. It is always one of those things that I am quite proud of: I always managed to choose the right one.

We chose Megadeth, Nuclear Assault, Dark Angel, Possessed, Exodus – and the bands that I passed over you never heard of again. But with Megadeth, the record [Killing Is My Business... And Business Is Good!] came up, and I thought, "What a fantastic title! This is great. This is like Metallica. I can't lose." We put it out and we did very, very, very well with it. Then we were gong to do the second album. We had a contract for the second album. It was called, Peace Sells... But Who's Buying? We did some test pressings.

Then, suddenly, Combat told us that they had sold the contract to Island. "Island?! They do reggae and pop!" It just made no sense whatsoever.

About six weeks later I had a phone call from the main guy at Island saying, "Could you come over for a chat?" He said, "Look, we have this band. I think you know them – Megadeth."

"Yeah. Yeah, I know 'em."

And he said, "Well, we haven't got a fucking clue what to do with them. Can you put the record out for us – and we'll give you the record for free. You put it out and give us a royalty, and, you know, if you can break them, then we will do the next record."

We put it out, and the record did 60,000 – nearly 70,000 in the UK, and we handed them back a hit act. We did the same with W.A.S.P. at EMI. When they did 'Animal (Fuck like a Beast)' the EMI shareholders nearly had a cardiac arrest. EMI's management phoned me up and said, "Look, would you like to put this out for free? We are having nothing to do with it. If you get done by the obscenities people then it's your hard luck."

I said, "Yeah, bring it on. I'll have a go." We sold 250,000. It was in the chart for 14 weeks. In those days, the majors just didn't understand how big a business there was in that type of music.

Harold O was a friend and fan of the band from the early days, and began documenting their shows with his camera. Here he offers his perspective on Metallica's formative years, and reflects on an exciting time for US metal.

How did you come to be Metallica's photographer?
HO: Through a couple of friends of mine – Brian Lew, who was a real big tip-trader on the underground scene, and a guy called Ron Quintana, who of course came up with the name of the band. I hooked up with them. I started contributing photos to their magazine, Metal Mania. They turned me on to Metallica when the first album came out. I photographed one of their shows at the Keystone Palace. I think it was '82-'83. The band happened

to like the pictures, and they ended up using a couple of shots on [Ride The Lightning]. I hit it off with them too. They liked to go out and drink a few, you know, as is well-documented.

So, you were part of the scene, and you were photographing other bands, were you?

HO: Yeah, pretty much. All the thrash bands – you know, Slayer, Exodus and anybody else that came to town. I didn't really do it on a professional level. It was more just for fun, but then things starting picking up. Metallica didn't know what my last name was; they just knew it started with an O, and so when the time came to put a credit on the album, they just put Harold O, and it stuck.

What was special about them? How come it was them that you got involved with?

HO: They just had this stage presence, and taking photographs of them was easy, you know. It was hard to come out with a bad shot. They were playing the kind of music that no one had played before, and there was just this unbridled energy on stage. When they did their first shows, they would drink massive amounts of alcohol before they played, and so they would be totally smashed on stage. It was just this wild, drunken good time. The Bay Area was just a real happening scene back then, but a lot of the clubs have closed down now and it's not like it used to be.

The first concert that you went to – did you go there knowing that you would photograph them, or did you just happen to have your camera on you?

HO: It was kind of funny the first time I took pictures of them. There was a no-camera policy, and I ended up getting my film taken away by the security. They tried to expose the film, and I ended up getting it back. Luckily, I rewound it back into the camera, and took the shot that Cliff used on the album, which is funny because it nearly didn't exist. A couple of friends of mine from high school took photos of some of the shows. Back then you were allowed to take pictures at most concerts. You didn't have to have a photo pass; it wasn't big business like it is now – only during the first three songs, and all that baloney. Metallica usually played all three of the Keystones. There is one in Palo Alto, one in San Francisco, and one here in Berkeley. The San Francisco shows would always be the craziest, so I would go to the San Francisco shows to mosh, and the other two shows to take pictures, because the crowd was at lot mellower. The San Francisco shows were just off the hook – crazy, drunken bashes.

Why were they good to photograph individually? What could you capture of Cliff?
HO: Cliff would head-bang. The rest of the band would be going so fast, and he would be going at half speed. I could get some incredible shots of him with his hair sticking straight up in the air. Yeah! You couldn't get a bad photo of him. He was just an incredible bass player as well. I have never seen anyone like him to this day. He used loads of crazy effects – wah-wah pedals and stuff. I would time it so I would get the hair right at the top, as far as it would go. It's the conviction they had on stage. At first, James wasn't much of a front man, he wasn't very sure of himself, but through the years he's really gotten really good at that. Now he is very natural up there.

Was Dave ever in the band when you took photos, or were those years over?
HO: Yeah. There was one show at the Waldorf, the first time I saw him. I think it was The Night of the Banging Heads. I think that's what it was called. I took lots of photos of Megadeth as well, back when Kerry King [of Slayer] was in the band. That didn't last very long! Yeah, I feel very sorry for Dave, because

he's never lived [his time in Metallica] down, you know. Maybe [Megadeth] were great on their own, but they will always be in the shadow of Metallica, unfortunately.

Was there a different kind of charisma when Kirk [Hammett] joined the band?
HO: To a certain extent. See, when Dave was in the band, they were much more drunk on stage, and he did more talking too, until James got more sure of himself. You know, a lot of people thought that [Kill 'Em All] was wimpy compared to those early demos with Dave, and Dave accused Kirk of copying all his solos, which was true to a certain extent, but I thought that the album was spectacular. I mean, it's interesting to hear the difference between that and the demo. They couldn't be more different sounding. It's interesting that on Ride the Lightning they did a ballad, 'Fade to Black', and everyone said that that was a sell-out, too. I think that's some of the best stuff, those slower songs.

Can you remember any shows in particular, anything that was memorable? I mean, you photographed the Day on the Green?
HO: Yeah, The Day on the Green 1985. It was a huge show, one of the biggest that was ever done in the States up to that point. It was at the stadium in Oakland. They used four or five band bills, and Metallica got to play one back in 1985. It was Scorpions, Ratt, Y&T, and Rising Force, with Metallica second on the bill.

It was interesting, because in order to get one of the photo passes that they had, I had to do their dishes. They actually had me do their dishes at their house on Carlson Avenue in El Cerrito. As I found out later, they had more photo passes than they said. Still, they had me do their dishes, empty the garbage, and do a couple of other chores around the house. But it was a great show.

99

I got really, really drunk. I was so excited; I had never been backstage at a huge festival like that. I got really, really drunk, and me, James, and a couple of other people trashed the dressing room. I was taking huge avocados and throwing them through the air conditioning vents. Wham were supposed to play the next day, and they had to give George Michael a little tiny trailer off to the side. A few years later, James apologised to Bill Graham [the festival's organizer]. There's a classic photo of James and Bill Graham, and James has this look on his face. There was a huge party at their house afterwards.

Basically, they didn't like to drive to gigs, because they got so drunk, so I would drive them round, and ended up getting as drunk as they were. It's amazing nobody actually got killed – you know, that we made it this far. They used to have lots of big parties at their house in El Cerrito. They used to call it Metallica Mansion, so for a long time, I actually pictured it as this huge mansion, but it ended up that it was this small, ratty dive that they lived in. Day on the Green was especially fun.

So in those days, were they ever arrogant? They are rock stars now, really – if you know what I getting at. Were they ambitious?
HO: They were always serious when they had to be, you know, especially Lars. He was always the business-minded guy in the band. When it came to recording albums and doing shows they couldn't have been more professional. I knew them pretty well, so I didn't get much of an attitude from them. I would say, up until maybe ...And Justice For All, they couldn't have been much more approachable.

It just seems to me that they were just having fun, almost not knowing where they were going...
HO: Yeah. I don't think that they thought it was going to get as big as it got, you know. They were always professional. I saw

Lars do a couple of things, back in the day, that were kind of rock star-ish, you know. He broke somebody's camera once.

I pretty much just followed them around with a camera – hounded them constantly. They were pretty co-operative most of the time, and I would always give them copies of the photos and stuff. I did a shoot with Kirk and James – they were both in bed together with all their guitars. It was supposed to be this humorous thing, and I guess I wasn't really supposed to print or publish any of the photos from that shoot, because there were some personal ones. James had a private, personal archive, you know. Ron Quintana ended up using one of his pictures on the cover of his magazine and James was kind of upset at the time. We got, like, into a bit of an argument and he said, "You're not taking photos of us any more ..." blah-blah-blah. How was I supposed to know he was going to use it as a cover shot? They still allow me to take photos of them.

Was that perhaps an early indication that they are actually quite ambitious? They are not really vain and brash anymore, are they?
HO: No. Not at all. I mean, the thing that was so interesting to me was that in Europe, they were huge. They were playing at big festivals with 40,000, 50,000 people. Then, here, they would come back and play tiny clubs. Europe is much more hip and catches on to stuff quicker.

The New Year's Eve show. What was that like?
HO: Master of Puppets was just about to come out, and they played a big New Year's Eve show at the Civic Auditorium. It was Metallica headlining, with Exodus, Metal Church, and Megadeth opening. So I got to know all of those bands pretty well, and it was mayhem, going from one dressing room to another. It was interesting, because Megadeth were opening, and Metallica were top of the bill. They didn't really hang out

much. James and Dave, they never got along much after he got booted, you know, but Lars would always be hanging out. He was always the one that would try to break the ice.

Did he feel guilty?
HO: To a certain extent. I don't think that he realised how much the band meant to Dave, and for him to see how big they got must have been hard. I mean, Megadeth have sold nearly 20 million albums, and that's still pretty incredible, but I think that Dave is still bitter.

Have you seen Metallica play recently?
HO: I went to a rehearsal at the Cow Palace in 2004. That was pretty spectacular. They invited two or three hundred people, and they had a full stage show. It was really weird being in the Cow Palace with so few people there.

Why did they invite you to a rehearsal?
HO: Just to get some people there to feel the vibe, so it wasn't just like a practice. It was basically just a rehearsal for the upcoming show, so they had cues down. I guess so the lighting people could do all their lighting stuff, and the pyros.

Were they rehearsing for the St. Anger tour?
HO: Yeah, exactly.

What did you think of it?
HO: Oh, it was great! When there's a big crowd there, it dampens some of the explosions and stuff. When it's empty – oh my god, it's 10 times louder! I thought I would be blinded and deafened by that.

Their Fan Club has been fantastic to me. They hooked me up with VH1, who have used some of my photos more recently, so I would like to thank Vicky, head of the Fan Club, and Stefan Sherosi, who is editor of the magazine. They have been a huge help to me of late.

When did Metallica start to get really famous? When did they start to move out of the Bay Area and stop hanging out with all of you guys?

HO: It was really gradual. There was a point when we would still hang out, and I would still see them at shows and stuff – probably around when …And Justice for All came out. That was the coolest thing; they were so big, but they still took time out for us. I would see James at shows and he would buy everybody a round of drinks. It's interesting how I would bump into them in the strangest places sometimes. I worked in a photo shop in Berkeley here. It was the Christmas rush on the photos, and there was this huge line of people. All of sudden, there is Lars in line turning in his film. Little by little, we saw less and less of them at gigs. Now, of course, they have bodyguards and all that. There are some over-zealous fans.

Was James more introverted do you think? Did he come out of his shell? It sounds to me as if he was pretty normal!

HO: Yeah, for the most part. In the early days, he wasn't really sure of himself on stage. He was pretty guarded about his privacy, but once you got to know him, then he was the most loyal friend ever. Actually, after one show I was particularly drunk, and I drove them to their house and was about to drive home, completely smashed out of my skull, and he took me out of the car and made sure that I didn't drive. Like I said, it's amazing that nobody got killed. He's hard to get to know, but once you get to know him, he's the best friend. Lars was the only one that had attitude once in a while. Somebody asked him if he wanted cheese on a sandwich one time. He says, "Sure I want cheese. I could buy this whole goddam place!" or something like that.

What about Kirk? Did you know him very well?

HO: He was a little bit quieter. He was a big toy collector. Kirk was probably the shyest one of them all. I didn't hang out much with him.

When did they rehearse? Did they rehearse much?
HO: They rehearsed at their house, actually. They used to have an old one-car garage at the back, and they turned that into a studio. That's where they wrote the first two or three records. Of course, once they got a bit bigger, they moved out and got their own big studio.

Did you ever see them rehearse or take pictures of them jamming or anything like that?
HO: Yeah, a couple of times. James and Cliff had a side band; it was a stupid joke band called Spastik Children that they formed with Fred Cotton, one of James's best friends, a really rude and obnoxious fellow. He was the vocalist, James played drums, Cliff played bass, and they had a guitar player, James McDaniel. It was just horrible racket! I was at one of the practices, and Fred started to sing this song about me. It was called 'The Ballad of Harold O'. The lyrics were rather unflattering. The next thing you know, it became part of their set, and I would get all drunk, get up on stage and dance. Cliff wrote this really interesting bass line, and just because I happened to be there, Fred just started singing it: "Harold you're this, Harold you're that ..." I don't want to go into it in too much detail, but it was fun. The funny thing about Spastik Children was that a lot of people heard it was the guys from Metallica, and so they would go expecting something that resembled Metallica, and it was just this horrible noise, this spewage, punk rock, just garbage. It was great seeing people's reaction to it, and Fred would tell the audience, "I can't believe you guys paid 20 bucks to see us!" It started getting so big that, after a while, they had to put it on hold permanently because the word got out that it was those guys, and the next thing you know, the place is total riot, you

know. They practiced a couple of times at this place called the Rehearsal Spot in Haywood, and that's where they ended up trying out bass players when Cliff passed away.

Did you photograph them much after Cliff passed?
HO: To a certain extent, but not quite as much. They didn't hang out as much as they did before. I mean, a lot of photos I had taken of them were just pictures of them hanging at other people's shows. They allowed me access, though, which was great, because they had a couple of main photographers that did most of their stuff, like Ross Halfin – English gentleman. He was a total jerk. He was really controlling about the photo shoots, and he made it hard for me a couple of times. He fell out with the band after a while. He was a pompous English jerk, basically, but he was also my idol to a certain extent, because he had photographed Iron Maiden and a bunch of bands back in the day. I tried to get his autograph once, and he wouldn't sign.

I was wondering what Jason Newsted was like on stage. Did you take photos of him in comparison to Cliff, that kind of thing?
HO: Oh yeah, Jason was just ace. When he joined the band it was great, because he was a real strong personality himself. He was like a madman on stage, and he would run around. He always gave one thousand percent every night, and if there was anybody out after the show signing autographs, he was the guy. He went out of his way to be cool with people all of the time.

Jason just brought a whole different feel to the band. He played with a pick instead of his fingers, so some of the stuff is tighter, but, unfortunately, you can't really hear his bass at all on ...And Justice For All. If you look at the back cover of the album he looks kind of pissed about that. I think, yeah, they had trouble after Cliff died, but I think that they have recently accepted it, got some closure on it. Jason fitted in great. He's

got to be the most down-to-earth non-rock-star guy you could ever meet.

Have you seen them or photographed them since Robert Trujillo has been in the band?

HO: Yeah, the last three or four shows they did. They played at Candlestick Park, where the [San Francisco] Giants play, and they did the San Jose Arena. He's great. He is a great addition to the band. I mean, just personality and everything. I know him a little bit from back in the Suicidal Tendencies days, and of course when he played with Ozzy. He gave them a new lease of life, I think. At their most recent show, right in the middle of a set, James comes up to me while I am taking photos and sticks his hand out, as if to shake my hand. Eventually, I figure out that he wants me to hit his hand. He's not even playing the next riff for the next song. I'm holding up the whole show here! The stage shows are really interesting; they're basically in-the-round. They are still photogenic, and luckily there are no Ross Halfin-type people there. The guys are still pretty cool about giving me access.

Is there anything else you want to say Hal? Stories that I haven't tapped in on?

HO: I just want to thank the guys in the band for 20 fun years, and for being so cool and allowing me into their lives. I think it's great that they are still a good band. I have to say that I like their older stuff a little bit more than their newer stuff, but how many bands have gone on as long as they have and are still that popular? I think that, with Robert in the band, the new stuff is going to be great. He is going to have much more input, I think.

How does the fan club work?

HO: The fan club is amazing. I can't think of a band that has such a hands-on approach to the fan club stuff. They allow the fans tickets to shows before they go on sale, meet-and-greet things, and all that. They put out a magazine [So What!] every quarter; Stefan [Chirazi] is the editor. It's the probably the coolest fan club ever, as far as just staying close to the fans.

I heard that they invited fans to their auditions for a new bass player...
HO: Yeah. Basically they had a party for a bunch of contest winners and flew them from all over America, and as they didn't have a bass player at the time, they auditioned three or four people who got to jam with the band at their studios. I think that the best bass player of the day was a girl. She did fantastic with them. I can't think of another band that's so down-to-earth as far as being cool to their fans and everything, you know. They are pretty much number one as far as that goes.

Journalist and author Joel McIver is recognized as a leading authority on Metallica, as well as a huge fan. In this exclusive interview, he offers his critical perspective on the band's output.

What kind of debut was Kill 'Em All? Was it a turning point in the genre of heavy metal?
JM: Kill 'Em All was an interesting album because it was different from what had gone before. It was a lot faster and a lot heavier than much of the records that were around at the time, especially the stuff that constituted the New Wave of British Heavy Metal.

Another thing was that they, James [Hetfield] especially, had this unique picking-hand technique. It was extremely staccato and extremely precise, so it sounded different. The songs were aggressive and short, although they weren't particularly progressive.

It was a turning point in the metal genre because it was so fast and so raw. A lot of people found that a little bit hard to take, actually. Some people thought it wasn't polished enough. Some people thought it wasn't refined enough. On the other hand, a lot of people really got into it, just because it was so fast and so heavy.

Did it not sound very tuneful at the time? Does that make sense? I mean, I think that they are a very tuneful band...
JM: I think in the context of the time it did sound pretty raw. The production was pretty terrible when you look back on it. They didn't really have a producer who knew what he was doing, and they didn't have much of a budget, because Megaforce Records was brand new and didn't have much cash.

I think a lot of people regarded it as a bit of a noise, really. It was really fast, and they had all these hardcore punk influences which put the focus on the aggression rather than the on melody. I think that some people found it hard to take.

Who was listening to it, do you think?
JM: The audience for Kill 'Em All was composed of kids who were into the New Wave of British Heavy Metal, bands like Venom and Diamond Head that were coming out of the UK, and then also the stadium rock audience who, like Hetfield himself, had been listening to Ted Nugent, Aerosmith, and all those terrible bands of the seventies who had peaked and were on their way down.

How popular was 'Seek and Destroy' at the time of its release? I think that now it's pretty much a metal anthem. Has it got anthemic qualities, or did they develop over time?
JM: 'Seek and Destroy' was popular live because it had that call and response section that James could exploit to get the crowd singing along. It's not the most exciting thing when you listen to the record, but live it really came into its own because James could do his thing. Funnily enough, it was one of those songs that saw him evolve with it as a front man. He was quite reserved before that, but when he had a bit that was tailor-made

for crowd participation it did him a lot of good as a performer, I think.

Is the album just all emotive sounds and phrases or are there contexts behind the songs?
JM: In a sort of naïve way, they do talk about warfare on a couple of the songs. 'No Remorse' and 'Metal Militia' are about going into battle, with troops of doom and all those clichés, but basically, what they are doing is knocking out a load of metal clichés. James himself has admitted as much. In 'Whiplash', there is the line, "Bang your head against the stage / Like you never did before / Make it ring, make it bleed / Make it really, really sore", which tells you something about the level of their songwriting in 1983.

A couple of people have mentioned that Cliff Burton was really pissed off about the fact that they couldn't call it Metal Up Your Ass. Were they the most extreme people on the scene or is it just that they are now the most well-known?
JM: You mean, extreme lyrically…?

Yes. I suppose, but also visually – what they wore, or what was on the album cover – what were they trying to achieve?
JM: You have to remember that at the time they were in their late teens or early twenties, so they were quite young when they were writing this album, and so some of the things are pretty juvenile. The whole thing about the original album sleeve, which was supposed to have a cartoon of a hand holding a knife coming out of a toilet, is just the sort of thing that you would do if you were 18 years old and you thought you had the fastest, harshest, heavy metal band in the world. All of that stuff hasn't really stood up as the years have passed.

Do you think that anybody thought that they were Satan's

spawn? It's hard to know now if they really were new and shocking, or if nobody was really listening.

JM: What was shocking about them was the music, really. It was much heavier and scarier than the lyrics, unless you happened to be 14 years old and you were blown away by those sort of the metal anthems.

The reason why Kill 'Em All made an impact was because it was fast and relentless. It really didn't slow down at all.

'Whiplash'. Is it straightforward, out-and-out thrash metal? Has it dated at all?

JM: 'Whiplash' is definitely pure thrash metal 1983 style. It's really unsophisticated, and you could play it if you'd been studying the guitar for six months, maximum – but it is very fast, and lots of fun to watch live. I think that it has remained perennially popular just because it is a bit of nostalgia, really. I mean, it's 20-plus years since it was recorded and written, and it does sound great live – not so good on the record, though.

The record generally – I know the production values were a bit crap. There are so many mistakes, aren't there? Does it sound like a live record almost?

JM: It's not that it's full of mistakes, but it's not perfectly executed. Basically, the sound of Metallica was forged on James doing this amazing rhythm guitar thing, where he would record one rhythm guitar track on the left, one on the right, and then put in what he called a thickener, which was a guitar track which sat on top of everything in the middle. He spent hours and hours in the studio – days, in fact – really perfecting it, making it tight. You don't really hear much of it on the first album, because they didn't know quite what they were doing. There is a rhythm guitar channel on either side, but it's just not quite as tight as on later albums, which is one reason why Kill 'Em All sounds a little bit garage-y.

113

Yeah. I think you can tell it's not done on Pro Tools, or whatever; they do speed up and slow down. It's like Motorhead's recordings, isn't it? It's quite …
JM: Organic!

Is that good or bad? Is that what's good about the debut?
JM: It has a really good feel, and it sounds very of-its-time. It sounds like they didn't have much money, but that does make it entertaining. The songs were so basic that you couldn't have really given them an enormously polished production.

Do you think there was much difference between the performances that Dave Mustaine and Kirk Hammett gave during the early days?
JM: Technically, they are both absolutely amazing guitarists. There was not an awful lot to call between them at that stage. Aficionados say that nowadays Mustaine has the edge in technical skill, but the difference between the sounds that they made back then was primarily that Kirk had this European influence. His heroes were UFO, the Scorpions, and all those great guitarists, so you could hear that slightly different flavour in his sounds. Mustaine is an amazing guitarist. I interviewed him a few years ago.

Did you?
JM: Yeah. A couple of times, actually. Entirely reasonable man, but he does tend to blame other people for his problems.

Yeah. Well I guess he has never been listened to though, really – if he had a shit upbringing?
JM: I think a lot of people don't take Dave seriously, but then, on the other hand, he has sold 15 million albums, you know. You can't go wrong with that.

Is he a big Christian now?
JM: Yeah – amazingly, yeah. His exact words to me were, "A

lot of people have made a big deal about the fact that I have found God, and it is a big deal, but I still say 'fuck' and I still like blow jobs."

He's just swapped one obsession for another?
JM: Exactly.

Who's the better rhythm guitarist, him or Hetfield?
JM: That's a really good question, actually, and a guitar geek like me could spend hours talking about that. Dave always described himself as this pioneer, and to a degree he was, because he could do these really, really twisty, complex things and come out on time. James had this approach that was just like an avalanche. He was unstoppable; he just wouldn't stop until the rhythm section was laid down and perfect, so that you couldn't tell one guitar track started and another one finished.

They were both geniuses in that field, really. James is actually a pretty fine lead guitarist as well as a bass player and a drummer. He played all the instruments on a Waylon Jennings cover he did a couple of years ago – fairly well as I understand it.

Are they similar at all?
JM: James and Dave?

Yeah.
JM: Well they have both been through rehab. One of the things that Dave said about the film [Some Kind Of Monster, a documentary following the recording of Metallica's 2003 album St. Anger] was, "How come James was given all this opportunity to go through rehab, whereas I wasn't? I was kicked out when my drinking got out of hand." The answer is because they are an incredibly rich band now, so they can take a year off for James to go into rehab, whereas back then they were 21.

What kind of a front man was James at this time? I am still thinking about all those early performances when you can't

really tell who is the voice of the band. They all seem to be shouting all of the time. Were they all finding their feet?

JM: In the early days, James didn't really have much confidence as a front man. At the very early gigs, Dave Mustaine used to do the talking, and I think from the first or second gig they ever did James even stood sideways on to the audience because he was afraid to look at them. There are all these famous stories – how Dave broke a string and it took ages to replace, and so on – so it's a little bit difficult to say who the voice of the band was back then, because James wasn't very confident about his singing, or his stage-craft. It did evolve. It just took a little bit of time.

So, Ride the Lightning, then – what kind of a follow up album was this?

JM: Ride the Lightning sounded as if it had been recorded by a completely different band. They used a professional studio; they went to Sweet Silence in Copenhagen, where Rainbow and a couple of other big rock bands had recorded, because they liked the sound that those bands had achieved at this studio. Then they had this producer, Flemming Rasmussen, who runs the studio there, and who really, really knew his stuff. Coupled with the fact that they had matured as song-writers and written these amazing songs which were incredibly precise and a lot more progressive and complex, they had a really good production as well. When you compare the two records side by side, they sound completely different.

Have they put an echo effect on the vocals? The vocals sound a little bit dated to me...

JM: There is some reverb on 'Fight Fire With Fire', when he goes, "What the hell is this world coming to?" You think it sounds dated?

Have I imagined that?

JM: It sounds like an 80s album, for sure.

Why does it sound like an eighties album? Is it the production, or is it the song writing, or what?

JM: You remember all of those horrible splashy snare sounds that Phil Collins had? Metallica didn't have that exactly, but they did have an element of it, where there was a longer sound, a longer decay on the snare. There is a little bit of treatment to the vocals and the guitar. The whole sound of Ride the Lightning is really very soft. It's not an abrasive sound, and it's very, very polished. It's very, very warm, as if it is in the distance. That's something which was symptomatic of that era and the contemporary recording techniques.

Yeah. I don't think I mean echo; I think it sounds quite glassy. Like Foreigner...

JM: Which song are you thinking of?

All of them!

JM: Oh, I think the vocals are good.

Oh, they're not bad – they have a hollow sound, like Peter Gabriel's vocals. It's not echo?

JM: I think the vocals were recorded pretty dry, without many effects, actually.

Maybe it's the first track, then?

JM: 'Fight Fire With Fire'?

Maybe it sounds dated because they don't do it live very much, do they?

JM: No, it's too fast for them now! They can't play it any more, very well. 'Fight Fire With Fire' is an incredibly fast song. It probably remains the fastest one they have ever done, just in terms of pure picking speed, and they didn't play it very often because it really takes a lot of skill and a lot of dedication even to get warmed up enough to play that tune. On the other hand, they could probably settle down to rehearse for a few days and

get it nailed, but I think they have got better things to do. I would love to see them play songs like 'Fight Fire With Fire' more often, because they are very fast, excellently written, and very exciting to watch.

'Fade to Black'. Is this Metallica's first and finest ballad?
JM: 'Fade to Black' is certainly Metallica's first ballad, although you could argue that 'The Call of Ktulu', on the same album, has balladic elements. Whether you think it is their best ballad is a matter of taste. They have only done about three or four. A lot of people think that 'Nothing Else Matters' is the best. 'Fade to Black' is all right, actually. It's depressing, it's dark, but it's beautifully played. It has all these uplifting acoustic guitar sections. It's a wonderful piece of writing.

There has always been a tradition in metal of these bands dropping the metal act for a few minutes and putting in an acoustic ballad somewhere. They have all done it somewhere in their catalogue. I think that Metallica happened to do it very well, because they were consummate musicians by this point in their careers, especially the guitarists, and as song-writers they were ambitious. The logical result of that is that you end up with a ballad-y song, but with these metal elements.

'For Whom the Bell Tolls'. Is this indicative of the writing style they would later employ for the black album?
JM: 'For Whom the Bell Tolls' is this stripped-down heavy-metal song, with no pretences to thrash metal. It was a simple riff, all in E, the bottom drone that Metallica always used, and it pointed directly to the sort of stripped-down sound that they would employ for the black album and after that. That's one reason why it is a live anthem. It's simple; everybody knows it. It's got all these fun parts, like the distorted bass solo at the start, which Cliff put down, and the other bass players have copied very well. It is an amazing solo towards the end. It's a short

song, easy to digest, but it's one of the epic tracks on Ride the Lightning, for sure.

It almost finishes too quickly, doesn't it?
JM: Yeah, it's only about three minutes.

It's interesting what you were saying about the E drone. How do they achieve those sounds?
JM: In the eighties certainly, Metallica had a classic metal sound. Nowadays, most metal guitarists have what they call a scooped sound, which means that they boost the bass and the treble and reduce the middle so that you end up with a scooped profile on the graphic equalizer, leading to a very recognisable modern metal sound. Now, in the eighties you didn't really have much of this; Metallica had a very rounded, full sound that left lots and lots of space for the bass and drums and the other elements of the band.

Do they detune their guitars?
JM: Now they do. They tune down, yeah.

To what, E?
JM: In the 80s, most of the classic metal songs were in E, the default tuning of an electric guitar, but as the years have passed, bands have experimented with tuning lower and lower, because it gives you a heavier sound, especially live. Live, Metallica could tune down more and more. You can even get seven-string guitars which have a low B string for that extra-deep tone. In the eighties, certainly, they more or less confined themselves to the classic E, like so many other bands. Megadeth did the same.

It's very heavy. Even in my mind when I am playing these songs, it is a weighty riff? Why is that? Is it because they are all playing in unison?
JM: It's crushing, yeah. Metallica achieved this very heavyweight sound partly because of the expert bass playing,

and particularly because Lars had a good right foot. There was lots and lots of quite heavy bass drum in the sound. Largely, it was down to James, who would record several rhythm-guitar tracks, and the producers that they used, who knew exactly how to make it sound really, really heavy.

'Creeping Death' – is it a good example of how Metallica set themselves apart from other metal bands?

JM: 'Creeping Death' combined a lot of classic metal elements. It had this amazing lyrical subject, the biblical plagues of Egypt, which was just fantastic. Then it had this riff in it, which was highly catchy; it wasn't quite thrash, but it certainly wasn't mainstream metal. If anything, it had more in common with Iron Maiden than other metal bands of the day, like the Dio-fronted Black Sabbath. It's definitely one of the best songs on Ride the Lightning, and it has this incredible solo in it, which Kirk refers to as one of his favourites. It has an amazing tapping section at the end, and then this incredible pyrotechnic explosion, which marks it out as one of the high points of the record, easily.

Why is it a live favourite?

JM: Audiences love 'Creeping Death' because it has this stop-start riff that they can get into, and it builds for 30 seconds at least before the main riff comes in. There is an amazing tempo change, but it is quite a rapid song when it does get going after this slow build-up, and they do all sorts of interesting stuff with it live. Kirk throws in an amazing solo. It's old school, and people love that stuff. They obviously like playing it as well. It's not like they are trotting through an old song just because they think they should. They all enjoy playing it and I think that the energy transfers to the crowd.

Is Ride the Lightning full of killer tracks?

JM: Ride the Lightning is definitely one of the classic metal albums of the eighties, for sure. There is no getting around it.

I'm trying to think what else is worth mentioning?
JM: On that album in particular?

Yeah?
JM: There is that epic instrumental, 'Call of Ktulu'.

Was that weird at the time?
JM: Yeah, it was a little, bit strange. 'Call of Ktulu' was a slightly odd song because it was an instrumental, to start with, and it mixed in all of these Metallica elements. It starts off with this beautiful, clean, picked guitar figure, which builds into this enormous mountain of riffs and just keeps on going. You think it's going to end, and it never does. It's not really loaded with solos, it's much more an exercise in James's rhythm guitar than it is Kirk playing lead. Even the title is taken from H.P. Lovecraft. It's classic 1984 metal.

Is Ride the Lightning the stand-out track?
JM: No. Ride the Lightning is a great song, but it's not the best song on the album – although it is an early Metallica classic. The whole concept of riding the lightening comes from someone who is sitting on an electric chair; it is quite appropriate to the darkness and depth of the record. When you think about 'Fade to Black' and 'Creeping Death', you realise that the whole album is about death and decay and depression, but it's actually a really thrilling record.

There are a couple of weaker tracks on that record...
JM: Yeah. 'Trapped Under Ice', and that really shit one, 'Escape'. 'Escape' has this anthemic vocal section towards the end, which must have been deliberately written as an attempt to make a hit single. No one has ever confirmed that they wanted to write a commercial song, but at the time, every journalist who reviewed the album said that 'Escape' was a little bit nauseating, because it has that sort of fists-in-the-air moment

which you would associate more with a band like UFO or Scorpion – the sort of band that wanted to please the crowds in the stadium.

There is a big jump from Kill 'Em All to Ride the Lightning, and from Ride the Lightning to Master of Puppets. Do they play like stepping stones or what?
JM: There is a leap in sophistication between each of the first three albums, certainly. Kill 'Em All was fairly raw. Ride the Lightning was very polished, but still had some of the classic themes. Then Master of Puppets was this epic record which was almost perfect on every single level. Later on, with ... And Justice For All, it seemed like they had become over-sophisticated, which I think is why they pared down their sound for the black album, which of course made them all millionaires.

Master of Puppets is arguably the album where everything came together.
JM: There were two things about Master of Puppets which make it essential if you are a Metallica fan. The first thing was the songwriting. Metallica had reached a point when they wrote songs which were still rooted in thrash metal – there is plenty of old-school fast stuff on that album – but also had this expanded palette, so you had these progressive sections which were quite inventive and quite experimental. The second thing about Puppets was that all these amazing songs would have been nothing if they hadn't had this really killer production, and Flemming Rasmussen, who once again produced the album at Sweet Silence in Copenhagen, did a great, great job. It is phenomenally heavy, and even in the faster selections, like 'Disposable Heroes', which is unbelievable rapidly picked, the production is still clear and precise, so that you don't miss out on any of it. It's really listenable. When you combine great songs and great production, that's 90% of a great album.

There is space on the album, actually, isn't there?

JM: Yeah, there is. One of the things that Lars said later on, when they recorded …And Justice for All, was that Puppets sounded as if it was coming from two metres behind the speakers, which is a result of the mixing rather than the actual recording, but he is right, there is a lot of space on that album, a lot of space to breathe. If you look at the song 'Orion', which breaks down at least twice into a smaller solo section, there is tons and tons of air that you can hear. It's really atmospheric.

Is he using one of those electronic drum kits?

JM: No, it's acoustic drums.

How did he do that, then?

JM: I think it's basically because he plays like a metronome, that's all. It's the playing that makes it sound like a drum machine, but no – drum machines were blasphemy, and an enemy to bands like Metallica in the '80s!

I was just checking on that. I'd never noticed it before, and then I thought, god, it isn't, is it?

JM: There are quite a few electronic effects on that album. The intros of both 'Orion' and 'Damage Inc.' were played by Cliff on his bass, which is heavily treated with effects. It's interesting at the beginning of 'Orion' because you have these layers of bass, which are treated with a chorus, one of those effects that were made popular in the '80s. The intro of 'Damage Inc.' has this reversed bass pattern - they recorded it, processed the sound and then reversed it.

Is 'Master of Puppets' a masterpiece and an outstanding track? Is it one of their more complex compositions?

JM: 'Master of Puppets' was a bit like their 'Bohemian Rhapsody', really, because it was composed of all these sections which sat back to back. Specifically, there was an instrumental bit in the middle with a clean-picked guitar part from James and a melodic solo over the top, a duelling harmony thing, from Kirk. It's one of their more ambitious songs, but unlike on their next album …And Justice For All, they kept the experimentation reined in, so it's not especially complex, but complex enough to retain your interest. If they'd made it an incredibly detailed and progressive experimental song, it wouldn't have been the live favourite which it's always been.

Is it complicated because it doesn't sound like a song? I mean, the structure is quite bizarre, isn't it? What is its charm?
JM: Well, it has a riff which sounds a little bit more complex than it is. It has a key change from E to F# as well, which elevates the tension. There is a sort of a stop-start section in the chorus. where James is shouting "Master, Master". The

vocal line duplicates the guitar line, so it sounds like a complex tune, but actually when you listen to it a few hundred times and break it down to its basic elements it's just a classic bit of metal songwriting, no more than that.

What characterises the Cliff era? Is this the album that has Cliff stamped all over it?

JM: Although Cliff's bass isn't necessarily any higher in the mix on Puppets than it is on the previous albums, his songwriting influence is all over it. You have to remember that by this point Cliff had been in the band for three years, and in that time he had been teaching the other guys the rudiments of musical theory; he was a trained pianist, you see. He studied Bach, and he studied all sorts of classical theory. He then passed those lessons on to James and Lars. On the other hand, he had this hardcore punk thing going on as well – he was a big Discharge fan – and so those influences filtered down to James and Lars, who were the primary songwriters.

On Puppets, specifically, the areas that Cliff excelled in were the more complex instrumental parts. So 'Orion', which was basically his song, starts with a bass solo and breaks down to a bass solo in the middle, which is a sort of a classical figure. Then he wrote this amazing, soaring, bluesy guitar section for Kirk to solo over just after the middle section. You can hear this epic flying section of guitar, which is solely down to this musical education.

Why does he look like Mick Ralphs out of Bad Company?

JM: Cliff had an amazing image for 1982. He had these big wings of hair that sort of fell down and hid his face, but he also insisted on these flared jeans, which in 1982 was just blasphemy for anybody who was interested in fashion – and the band took the mickey out of him day by day, but he never cared. It was one of these things that made him who he was.

Why didn't that matter?

JM: It was highly uncool to look the way he did, but any detractors he might have had shut up quickly and stopped laughing when they saw how well he could play, how well he wrote his songs, and how phenomenally heavy Metallica were at this point. There was no arguing with them, no matter what they looked like.

'Battery' is an amazing song. It starts with this phalanx of acoustic guitars, similar to those that begin Ride the Lightning. This time, what Rasmussen had done was build this massive wall-of-sound to introduce the album. The song itself is based on this twisty riff, which is quite clever and quite hard to follow, but a stroke of genius really, and one which they didn't really replicate too easily on some on their later albums.

'Disposable Heroes' is the high point of Master of Puppets for that portion of the old-school-fan-base fans who are obsessed with speed and heaviness for its own sake. It's a really, really fast song, based on a chord progression that James has used and re-used, notably on 'Eye of the Beholder' from ...And Justice For All. It is just amazingly fast, with an amazing solo in the middle. They never play it live, which is a real shame, and I don't know why.

'Welcome Home (Sanitarium)' is one of the band's most popular live songs. It starts with this very down-tempo, clean-picked guitar intro, complete with guitar harmonics; it's a nice piece of guitar playing. Then it goes into this strange 5/4 time signature with a brilliant bass line from Burton. The song does the classic Metallica thing of going into a fast heavy section halfway through, and then explodes into the big pyrotechnic ending.

They also did a song called 'The Thing That Should Not Be', which is amazingly heavy. It's a slow song, but it has to be slow because it is so – so heavy. I don't know how far they tuned down but… It is based on some sort of Lovecraft mythos, another great bit of ridiculous metal writing, rather like Creeping Death on the previous album.

Does that sound more like the black album?
JM: There are similarities between slow songs on Puppets, like 'The Thing That Should Not Be', and then the stripped-down, more rock-radio songs on the black album, but Puppets is much heavier; it drags itself along. There is nothing radio-friendly about 'The Thing That Should Not Be'.

'Leper Messiah' is an interesting song, with lyrics that deal with the ridiculous phenomenon of US TV evangelists. It is full of these images of stinking, leprous, gangrenous people, which served to illustrate the themes quite well. It was quite imaginative songwriting, actually. Again, it is a slow song, but has this fast section in the middle, which is what the old-school fans hungered for, and it went down really, really well.

Is Master of Puppets about heroin?
JM: Coke. There is a line, "Chop your breakfast on a mirror." At the time you couldn't be open about these things. They didn't really say what it was about until much later on, but it was apparent to everybody that they were talking about cocaine. The master of puppets is the controlling element of an addiction.

The last song, 'Damage Inc.', is another one of my favourites. It's a really, really fast, really, really exciting song that harks back to their thrash roots. What we are dealing with here is a thrash metal band of enormous power, at their peak.

Were they at the top of their game do you think, when Cliff died?
JM: When Cliff died, Metallica were at an incredible song-writing peak, partially because Cliff himself was a fantastic song writer, and although Lars and James were the primary songwriters, he did contribute a lot. When he died, there was an

opportunity for them to take over the whole of the songwriting, and when that happened we saw the changes in direction which resulted in the black album and their commercial peak.

What were they doing with Garage Days? Was it an unusual thing to do?

JM: The recording of the Garage Days EP was a chance to showcase [new bass player] Jason Newsted's skills. That's why they recorded it. It also served to promote their appearance at the 1987 Donington Festival. It was a slightly unusual move, partly because of the songs that they covered, which were mainly from the New Wave of British Heavy Metal. There was a song by Holocaust, one by Diamond Head, and also a Killing Joke track. The Garage Days EP sounded amazing, perhaps because they didn't fool around with the production for too long. In fact, I believe on the record it says "not produced by…" One of those Metallica quips.

So, how well did they do punk?

JM: Metallica have recorded various punk songs, and to me they did it by numbers really. They don't have the punk edge; they don't have the punk rawness. Their aggression is entirely of the metal school. Nonetheless, it is do-able. Quite a few bands have attempted it. Megadeth did a cover of 'Anarchy in the UK', and Slayer recorded a whole album of punk covers in 1996 [Undisputed Attitude]. It can be done, but it doesn't really compare to the original stuff.

Is it an excuse to be a bit outrageous, do you think?

JM: I think that the first time Metallica played 'So What' [a song originally by Anti-Nowhere League, a British punk outfit] in public was the MTV award ceremony, I think. It was really just an attempt to show people that they were still quite young and controversial. A lot of the English fans didn't like the song really that much. They replaced two instances with the 'C' word

129

with the 'F' word, to placate the American audiences, I think, who might have found it a little too much.

'Breadfan'. Why choose this song, because it's quite blues? What does it show about them?
JM: 'Breadfan' showed that, when Metallica want to, they can record a cover that is actually an improvement on the original. Budgie's 'Breadfan' was a great song, but it wasn't recorded particularly well, and didn't have an awful lot of aggression. When Metallica did it, their version was amazing, absolutely incendiary. It's really, really fast and precise, as always, with this old-school, slightly bluesy element.

What informs the album ...And Justice for All? Are the lyrics much darker on this record?
JM: The lyrics, for the first time, dealt with political and environmental issues. There were a few other bands at the time, like Nuclear Assault, who were applying ecological lyrics to thrash metal, but this [on 'Blackened'] was the first time that Metallica had ventured into such territory. They also talked about political corruption, and although they didn't allude to any particular institutions, it was apparent that rather than singing about Satan and Egyptian plagues they were singing about subjects that were much closer to home.

Where is the bass on the record?
JM: I interviewed Jason a couple of years ago for my book and he told me that, while ...And Justice For All was being mixed, they were touring with the Monsters of Rock festival, with Van Halen and the rest of them, and in between shows James and Lars were driving down to the studio where the album was being mixed.

At one point they said to the engineers, "Take the bass down so you can barely hear it, and then knock a decibel off the top of that."

So I said to Jason, "Why would they do this? You know, you are a great bass player," and apparently they said that they had a multitude of reasons.

Allegedly, they weren't too confident about his skills when he replaced Cliff, and secondly, there was a slight click because his plectrum was hitting the stings. That seems stupid to me, because you can take that out anyway, in the production. So it would seem that they didn't really want his presence to be felt on the album. Of course, you could spin it the other way and say that the guitar sound which James used on the album was so vast that in fact it was appropriate to take out the bass frequency space. It is endlessly debatable, and we will never really know what happened, unless they decide to talk about it, or indeed reissue a re-mastered remixed version of the album with the bass line in it. That would be all right.

I wonder if the reason why they removed the bass is because it was too complicated with it in? There must be a reason...
JM: I think, basically, they removed the bass because James's guitar took up the frequencies that the bass normally fills. I interviewed Christian Olde Wolbers of Fear Factory not long ago. He is an amazing bass player and an amazing guitarist, so he knows. His theory is that because James's guitar playing and those riffs were so incredibly precise, yet so heavy, the fact that there was a bass on the album at all meant that it was intrusive, so they had to take it out. It's just one possible opinion, but we'll never know until James or Lars tells us.

'One' is a bit of a sprawling epic. Do you think that song is generally a little overblown? Are there interesting moments?
JM: 'One' is a good song to listen to, but it doesn't really break any particularly new ground, because they had done a half-ballad-half-thrash before. There is an element of conceit in the inspiration they drew. The subject is a man who has been

injured on the battlefield and lost his limbs, inspired by the anti-war novel, and subsequent film, Johnny Got His Gun, so you can kind of forget the lyrics really. It's not terribly convincing when James is singing from the viewpoint of someone who's in a hospital and wishes to die, but the song itself, you can't knock it. The first section does go on quite a lot, but when it actually takes off and speeds up it's an amazing song, it's very well produced, and very well played.

Is the problem that it doesn't hang together very well? Personally, I find Lars's drumming way too complex.
JM: In the mellow section?

I'm not sure. I just find it distracting. Is there anything to say about Lars's drumming in general on this album? Is it any different to normal?
JM: Lars has never been credited as being the best drummer ever. Nonetheless, that shouldn't take away from the fact that he is a highly competent drummer. One thing that does annoy a few people is that occasionally he doesn't know when to lay back and take it easy. An example might be the first section of 'One', which is supposedly a melodic quiet section, which he could've played down a little bit. There is another song, on Reload, called 'The Unforgiven II', which is extremely quiet and mellow in its first section, and Lars is all over the place, hitting the snare, he could have done some rim shots, just to keep it down a little bit, but that's his style.

'Harvester of Sorrow' starts with a catchy riff, but is the song rather pedestrian? Is it a bit too long? Is it the hardest track on the album?
JM: No. 'Dyer's Eve' is harder. I think that 'Harvester Of Sorrow' was chosen as the first single from Justice because it is fairly catchy, it's not too intimidating, and it's moderately radio-friendly – but it does go on a bit and doesn't really stand

up awfully well live. Nonetheless, it was a relatively useful introduction to the Justice album.

Do you want to hear some good things about it?
JM: People slag off the Justice album a lot, but I actually think it is time people gave it a second chance. The production and the mixing is suspect, okay, but, on the other hand, if you want a huge guitar sound, it's there for you. James's guitar sound fills all the frequencies, including the bass, unfortunately. When songwriting isn't too complex and too elaborate, then it can actually be quite pleasing. 'Dyer's Eve', for example, is basically old-school thrash. It is very similar to 'Damage Inc.' on the previous album, except that it doesn't have that attractive, rounded sound.

Justice is more of an album to be listened to, say, on a long train journey. It's something for when you're not in a hurry. You don't want to jump up and down to it because it doesn't really have that kind of sound, and doesn't really have those songs that make you want to jump into a mosh pit, but it has its place.

What's the stand-out track?
JM: 'One'.

Why was that not released first?
JM: Possibly the band thought that 'One' was a bit too aggressive to be released as the first single, and they wanted 'Harvester of Sorrow' to show that they now had a different, slower, more complex approach to the band.

I don't like it. It's really pedestrian. It's an uneasy album, though, isn't it?
JM: Totally, yeah.

The black album [otherwise known as Metallica] – how much of a surprise was the black album?
JM: The black album took everybody by surprise [in 1991],

although in retrospect we should have really known that, after the over-sophisticated approach of ...And Justice for All, they would strip it down and go for a more approachable feel on their next record. I don't think anybody expected it to sell as well as it did, or to receive as much MTV or radio exposure, but when you look back on it, and it's more than 15 years ago now, it was the obvious thing for Metallica to do at that point in their careers.

Is 'Enter Sandman' the stand-out track on the black album, or is just the most famous one? Is Bob Rock responsible for the pop element, or did they always have it in them?
JM: 'Enter Sandman' isn't necessarily the best song on that album, but it's very recognizable. It's very humble, and that was really a first for Metallica. What Bob Rock did was beef up the sound; there is a full bass presence. He made it radio-friendly. You have got to remember that he worked with people like Mötley Crüe and Cher before he worked with Metallica. He knew how to make an album sound good on MTV, through a little TV speaker or radio or whatever, so really he facilitated their desire to write simpler songs effectively. People blame Bob Rock for too much. It's not like he sat down with them in the songwriting room and said you can't do this, you have got to do that, but he did give them a very nice mainstream sound.

I mean, is that a bad thing, anyway? Surely, it was part of their talent...
JM: I think that their talents deserved to come through. In a way, the black album is highly listenable, you know. It took them a year to record for a reason, and it came out sounding really good. The songs are not particularly threatening, experimental, or progressive, but maybe after five albums, that wasn't what people wanted from Metallica any more.

Kirk's guitar sounds different on this album, particularly on 'Enter Sandman'. He sounds more like Slash to me.

JM: In the solo? There is a lot of wah-wah, which I suppose is quite Slash-y. More shred – shreddy? I don't know whether I can agree with that, really. It sounds commercial. The whole album sounds more commercial than what came before it, and that was down to Bob Rock and the songwriting, and includes things like Kirk's guitar sound.

Hetfield's vocal delivery on 'Sad but True'. Is this his strongest yet? I mean, it does sound quite poignant. How does it work?

JM: First of all you have this massive down-tuned guitar riff which was sampled by Kid Rock [in his song 'American Badass'] a few years later. Also, James has a very staccato, percussive, forceful vocal, which comes through. It's not over-complex. He's basically shouting words like "hate" and repeating them in an anthemic sort of way – definitely one of the high points of the album.

Is this the first album we actually hear him singing?

JM: Yeah, I know what you mean. Yes, James adopts a sung style rather than a shouted or barked vocal style on 'Nothing Else Matters' and then 'The Unforgiven'. While it wasn't badly sung, it was a bit a shock for most people because he had this crooning element to his voice, which was completely new for most people. A lot of old-school fans ran screaming when they heard that.

What's going on with Lars's drumming on the album?

JM: Lars chose to play simpler drum patterns to complement the simpler songs. If he hadn't it would have sounded bizarre. So he laid back, played simple beats, and that paid off in songs like 'Sad but True', where he has an enormous snare sound.

I wonder if it was hard work?

JM: For Bob Rock it would have been! And I think that the engineer, Randy Staub, deserves a lot of credit.

I wonder if it would have been hard work for Lars to chill out, as he obviously likes playing complicated things...

JM: I interviewed him last year. He is hard work! A nice guy, but tiring – like having a small, hyperactive puppy.

He's quite intense, isn't he?

JM: I interviewed Lars last year, for Metal Hammer magazine, and one of the things he told me was that he is a worrier. It's possibly one of the reasons why Metallica have done so well. He's pushed them very hard. Possibly one of the reasons why it's not his style to lay back and play a quiet, relaxed beat is that he has to go at it with all guns blazing.

He is quite driven, isn't he, like his tennis-playing father? Has he had to forge his own career?

JM: His dad is great. You ought to get him on – Torben Ulrich.

Does he still consult his father on music?

JM: I don't think he ever has consulted him. I think that was just a one-off for that film [Some Kind Of Monster].

Okay – because that was weird but interesting!

JM: I asked him about that. He just said that it was misconstrued by the public. His old man often chucks in comments like, "It isn't as good as that," or, "This could be better." It's not that Torben is regularly consulted on the music.

Yeah. It was a weird scene...

JM: The whole film was weird.

'Wherever I May Roam' – What did you think of this song? It sounds like a rehash of lots of other songs to me.

JM: 'Wherever I May Roam', funnily enough, was mooted as the first single off the album. Only Lars, as he explained later, could really see that 'Enter the Sandman' should be the first single.

Anyway, I can see why it has its commercial charms, but to me it's not a great song. It's fairly symptomatic of the black album, in that it's big, chunky, and singable, but not particularly memorable.

Is 'Nothing Else Matters' Metallica's best ballad?
JM: 'Nothing Else Matters' will certainly be the ballad for which Metallica are remembered. It's the song that introduced Metallica to the wedding video. Couples had their first dance to it, and that was quite exciting. It's quite a romantic song, actually, and if you can stomach the fact that this intense thrash metal band of yore are now doing this mellow ballad, then it's not a bad song. I wouldn't want to hear it too many times. Actually, its one redeeming feature is that it has a great solo in it, which James did himself. It's one of the best.

Does it grate a bit? Is it the kind of song that really ought to be delivered by another band?
JM: It was difficult for people to accept 'Nothing Else Matters'. It's quite a cheesy song, but it's symptomatic of Metallica's progression, and you either accept it or you don't. Metallica have always held the view themselves that you either come along with us for the ride or you don't.

Is the black album quite hard for them to perform? I'm just thinking about the vocals – I mean James' voice is screwed now...
JM: His proper metal voice...

Yeah?
JM: Yeah. He lost it in the early nineties.

Was it before this album? He sings quite well on the album...

JM: No, I think that they did a three-year tour off the back of that album, and that probably shredded his vocal chords. He can still sing, but it's just not the way it was. You've got to remember that he is older now, so maybe his vocal chords have just changed, and his style is different to the way it was.

I think that as the years have passed, James's voice has changed. I am not sure that he has the range now that he once had. Some of those early songs, like 'Eye of the Beholder' and 'Motorbreath', have the occasional high note that he can't quite hit, but I think that is quite typical of a lot of bands live, versus their studio performance. James's voice has changed. Everything about their live performances has changed. He doesn't have the same picking precision that he once had, the vocals are different, the drums are different, Kirk's solos are different – that's just symptomatic of a band that has been on the road for 20 years.

Are they a bit too old to be doing metal? Is that the problem?
JM: Metallica aren't too old to be doing metal, but they are not at their peak when it comes to performing really complex, fast, aggressive stuff, and I don't blame them for that. Lars said himself, in an interview recently, that he doesn't know whether he can still be performing really hardcore songs like 'Battery' and 'Disposable Heroes' when he is 50. Perhaps it's not reasonable to expect anybody to be doing that, you know. James Taylor and the Rolling Stones can go out and perform way into their fifties and sixties, but then they are not playing this sort of super-aggressive music.

Are they consistently brilliant live?
JM: Metallica have always been at their best on stage, and that's really what fans now have to cherish. No matter how good or how bad their studio albums may be, they always deliver a killer show live, and they have had a recent boost with the

recruitment of Robert Trujillo, who is an amazing showman. Jason Newsted was, as well. As long as they have got that kind of drive, and as long as they choose to tour, then I am sure they will be delighting people for years to come.

What characterised the eighties tours?
JM: One of the things that the black album did was turn Metallica from a club band into a stadium band. All right, they played stadium tours before the black album, but the shows were exclusively stadium-sized after it, apart from the odd little show, such as the one in '95 at the Ministry of Sound in London. They played these enormo-domes, and that, by definition, affects the show.

It means that they are more showmen-like now. Lars comes from behind the kit and runs around at the front, which is not traditionally the role of a drummer. James does far more of this fist-pumping, "Can you hear me on the left! Can you hear me on the right!" – the whole stadium shtick that they have to do. There's pyrotechnics. In '96 they had a whole collapsing lighting rig and a stuntman bursting into flames; he fell onto the stage and ended up being put out by firemen. It is more theatrical now.

I am not saying that they have turned into Kiss or Cradle of Filth, but the show doesn't have the hardcore serious edge that it had in the eighties. In the nineties they did funny little skits, jokes. Lars plays a bit of guitar. James does a bit on the drums. Okay, it's all good, but it's not quite as gripping and as serious and as forceful a show as it once was.

Why haven't Metallica stuck to a formula, like the other bands that came out the scene?
JM: Metallica have been provided with so much success that they can now do what they want, really. As a result, I think that they enjoy life. They do a funny show; they play the songs they

want to play; they travel where they want to go. But today, you don't go to a Metallica show to see a really, really intense, scary show, of the kind that you might see if you went to see Slayer, for example.

When did they change as a band?

JM: They did the alt-rock bluesy thing in '96 with Load. In 1995 and 1996 they had a change in direction. They changed their whole image [they cut their hair], which some people get right upset about, but I personally don't, because it's just an image. Alongside that, they changed their musical style. Load and Reload [the following year's sequel] were all about experimentation and toning down the heaviness. The alternative-rock thing was probably derived from the Seattle scene, which exploded in the early nineties.

What are the staples of their set? Do they have to avoid certain albums? Does their set show the peaks of their career?

JM: Nowadays, a Metallica set is not quite as shallow as a greatest-hit set, but it certainly does comprise the songs that people recognise. They have to play 'Master of Puppets', 'Battery', probably 'Creeping Death', then 'Sandman', 'Sad But True' and 'Nothing Else Matters' – the big songs off the big albums. They will throw in the odd tune that people don't expect – something from the Load and Reload era – but I think that they are aware that not everybody is really into those songs. They always play, say, 'St. Anger' and 'Frantic', certainly those two tunes from the most recent album, and then they will throw in an old classic like 'Am I Evil?'. I have to say that for the last few years the set lists have been, if not exactly predictable, then a fairly safe bet. I think that they have done a fairly successful job of actually appeasing everybody who comes to the shows – the new school, the old school, the slightly left-field songs, the unexpected tunes – they are all there.

What about their different bass players?

JM: Metallica have been blessed with their bass players ever since they got rid of Ron McGovney in 1982 and recruited Cliff Burton. Cliff, of course, had this incredible classical education. His grasp of music theory was second to none, and he translated that to the bass, so if you ever get to see a video of Cliff playing a bass solo, he throws in all these classical triads, there is all this Bach-influenced stuff, but with this incredible, raw, punkish overdrive applied to it.

Jason, while he was an amazing player, was never really given the chance to flourish. He did do a solo live, but his songs weren't really used on the albums. A solid, dependable player, definitely, who never put a foot wrong, he was so dedicated to getting those songs right.

Then we have the amazing Bob Trujillo, who honed his act with hardcore outfit Suicidal Tendencies. He had a funk project called Infectious Grooves, where he did all this slapping, popping bass style, very funky, and he was Ozzy's bass player for a while. I think the great thing about Rob is that he will drive them forward because he has this incredible energy, which I think they needed in 2000 and 2001 when they lost Jason.

The future?

JM: I think that Metallica will keep going for a few years yet. They are all in their early-to-mid-forties now. There is a question about whether they can continue to execute these very tough, demanding songs live, night after night, year after year. The question really is, as they are multi-millionaires now, do they want to? They all have side projects; they all have families – which is quite important to them – but, on the other hand, they have an enormous fan base which is happy to pay an enormous amount of money to see them play. On the other hand, I just can't see them playing this kind of music into their fifties. I can see them doing a semi-dignified thing and retiring to being a blues act, sitting on high stools playing acoustic guitars – that kind of thing, but who knows? Really, the question of whether they will carry on for much longer must be down to the quality of the music, the record sales, and whether they decide to go out on a high or not.

Is it an inflexible genre in that sense?

JM: What tends to happen in metal when bands are past their commercial peak – look at Deep Purple; look at the Scorpions – is that they tend to carry on playing the occasional tour, releasing the occasional record; not often playing a 500-night tour worldwide, but nonetheless still enjoying life and still doing things that are slightly slower and more dignified, at a less frenetic pace than previously. I imagine that Metallica, if they don't decide to just pack it in and quit, will follow that route.

Did you ever ask any of them what was their favourite moment in their career?

JM: I've only interviewed Lars and Jason. No, I didn't ask them that specific question.

I just wondered what seems to excite them most. Do they prefer recording or do they prefer the live?

JM: They are a live band. They are a live band for sure, and they don't like recording. One of the reasons why St. Anger was such a rushed album and sounds so odd was that they decided to get rid of the enormous extended production process that had hampered previous albums. But they are a live band and that's where their main strength is. All bands need a core strength, and theirs is live performance. I saw them in Newport on the Justice tour and it was amazing. They were super-tight in '87 and '88. Allegedly, they even faked the same mistake night after night on that tour. It was amazing.

Where was the mistake?

JM: I think it was a mistake by Jason in one of the songs towards the end of the set. He started it wrongly and they laughed at him and then carried on doing something else. They did it night after night, allegedly.

TRACK BY TRACK ANALYSIS

THIS TRACK-BY-TRACK run-through of Metallica's formidable recorded catalogue seeks to provide a clear, unbiased assessment of each of their songs and albums. Where a song is included more than once – on a single, live album or compilation as well as the parent album – I have indicated as such and referred the reader to the original entry.

Furthermore, with singles and live/compilation albums I haven't annotated each track, summing up the content with an overview: fuller analysis is reserved for original studio albums.

I've focused only on UK releases, as Metallica product from Japan, the USA and other territories came in a blinding array of variant formats and tracklistings.

I've given each song and album a rating out of five as follows:

★ ★ ★ ★ ★ - Absolutely essential
★ ★ ★ ★ - Excellent
★ ★ ★ - Average
★ ★ - Poor
★ - Terrible

Metallica are one of the few bands, metal or otherwise, who can boast an entire feature film dedicated to them – and I've included this too.

As most people know, Metallica's career can be divided into two halves – the critically acclaimed, progressive, groundbreakingly aggressive thrash metal of 1982 to 1990, and the huge-selling mainstream rock that has followed. While some fans enjoy both halves of the career equally, the majority do not – and this is reflected in the length of the entries for each song, which reduce in size after 1991. This isn't due to my own opinion; this is merely an acknowledgment of the social and artistic impact that Metallica once made, as opposed to the role they occupy now. Any assessment of – for example – the work of The Rolling Stones, REM, Iron Maiden, AC/DC, Paul McCartney and Britney Spears (to name six artists at random) might well do the same.

Tom King, 2006

POWER METAL
(Demo cassette, April 1982)

Tracklisting: Hit The Lights / Jump In The Fire / The Mechanix / Motorbreath

After six months of attempting to hone a sound, the all-teenage Metallica – James Hetfield, Ron McGovney and Lars Ulrich – recorded a demo in bass player McGovney's garage at 13004 Curtis & King Road, Norwalk, LA. The sound is rough but not quite as poor as some live recordings at the time: what stands out most is Hetfield's untrained wail and Lars' uneven snare pattern and amateurish fills. Still, hearing the young band is a revelation; James' rhythm guitar picking is clearly developing precision, while Ron's bass playing – usually written off as poor – is actually perfectly adequate. Note that Power Metal was not the original title – that was Jump In The Fire: the label came from a business card that Ron had printed at the time. A period piece, worth tracking down on the internet.

Overall rating: ★ ★

NO LIFE 'TIL LEATHER
(Demo cassette, July 1982)

Tracklisting: Hit The Lights / Jump In The Fire / The Mechanix / Motorbreath / Seek And Destroy / Phantom Lord / Metal Militia

A truly historical item, No Life 'Til Leather was copied by thousands of American metal fans and played endlessly through 1982, building a word-of-mouth reputation for Metallica that translated directly into album sales the following year. In fact, many viewed NLTL as superior to Kill 'Em All, thanks to the more melodic vocal style James employed on the tape, and the presence of Dave Mustaine, whose fiery leads hint directly at the phenomenal skills he would bring into play in Megadeth. High points are many, with the twisty riffing of Hit The Lights and The Mechanix pointing the way to the more technical songwriting that the band would employ in the next couple of years. Only Ron's plodding bass parts – quite a shock to anyone used to Cliff Burton's awe-inspiring performance on KEA – weigh the demo down. The lyrics for Jump In The Fire are different to those on the album, too, and just as well – the earlier version is a ludicrous sexual boast.

Overall rating: ★ ★ ★

KILL 'EM ALL
(Album, July 1983)

Tracklisting: Hit The Lights / The Four Horsemen / Motorbreath / Jump In The Fire / (Anesthesia) Pulling Teeth / Whiplash / Phantom Lord / No Remorse / Seek & Destroy / Metal Militia

Hit The Lights ★ ★ ★ ★
A proud statement of intent, Hit The Lights begins with a fade-in

(in which Cliff can be heard jumping around all over the place) and evolves into a speedy riff etched into James' crystal-clear, if slightly scratchy, rhythm guitar sound. The lyrics are juvenile but tap into the mentality of the nascent thrash metal movement, essentially at this stage a speeded-up version of standard braggadocio heavy metal. "No life 'til leather," squawks Hetfield, "gonna kick some ass tonight…" He would later look back on the lyrics with embarrassment, describing them at one point as "really stupid" – but nostalgic fans wouldn't have had it any other way.

Listen out for Kirk Hammett's excellent, extended solo at the back end of Hit The Lights: a perfect introduction to 'the new God of metal', as he was naively dubbed at the time.

The Four Horsemen ★ ★

A slightly overambitious attempt at progressive heavy metal without any real 'thrash' overtones, The Four Horsemen is a droning, longer-than-necessary song with too many bolted-together sections to make coherent sense after a few plays. However, it has its moments, namely the mellow section in the middle over which Kirk plays a slightly atonal solo. One noted metal journalist incurred Lars Ulrich's wrath by comparing this clean-picked section in a review to Lynyrd Skynyrd's Sweet Home Alabama, although the drummer apparently saw reason when it was pointed out to him that the descending arpeggios do in fact bear some resemblance to the Southern rock classic. Despite its occasional merits, The Four Horsemen wastes too much time droning along on a staccato E chord – accompanied by James' redundant screech of 'Oh yeah!" – to be a truly essential Metallica song for anyone other than completists.

Motorbreath ★ ★ ★ ★

Kill 'Em All takes a step upwards at this point. One of the finest early Metallica songs, Motorbreath sounds as if it were composed in five minutes and recorded in 10 – and is one of the most satisfyingly intense four minutes produced in the early thrash period. It's a mindless paean to life on the road – "Motorbreath, it's how I live my life / I can't make it any other way" intones James optimistically, having actually been on tour a total of no times at this point (unless you count driving from San Francisco to New York with the drunken Dave Mustaine at the wheel). Kirk is on majestic form here, taking a brief solo early on and an extended lead at the back end – and just listen to James and Cliff hit their rhythmic stride on an awesome D/C/D/ C/A riff that showcases their picking precision.

Jump In The Fire ★ ★ ★

Like Creeping Death and Welcome Home (Sanitarium) on subsequent albums, Jump In The Fire is a decidedly non-thrash song from this most resolutely thrash metal band – a song that rapidly became a live anthem thanks to its singalong chorus and its relative slowness, which allowed the crowd to punch the air without getting too tired. Lyrically a weak stab at the scary ol' Satanism that Slayer would perfect in due course, Jump is one of the catchier, even poppier songs that Metallica ever did (until the Load album, of course). Kirk's solo is an imitation of Dave Mustaine's arguably superior effort on the No Life 'Til Leather demo, droned intro and all, but is no less great for all that – and Cliff's bass part improves on Ron McGovney's original immeasurably by ascending to the octave at the end of every second bar.

(Anesthesia) Pulling Teeth ★ ★ ★ ★

Rather than being an actual song, Anesthesia... is a bass solo from Cliff Burton, in which he showcases his unique talents in the run-up to the album's key statement of intent, Whiplash. James or Lars is heard announcing "Bass solo, take one" through the studio mike before Cliff ignites his overdrive and distortion pedals and allows a chord to develop before launching into a triad pattern. In case you think I'm making too much of Cliff's bass playing on this album, bear in mind that it's the Metallica album on which his presence made itself felt the clearest – at least in performance, not composition, terms – and for obvious reasons his solo spot is where he shines most. Accompanied by Lars' mid-tempo drum pattern for the last couple of minutes, Cliff drags in a snatch of a Bach fugue before disappearing into an explosion of distortion and the sudden attack of the next song.

Whiplash ★ ★ ★ ★

Easily the most memorable song on KEA, Whiplash is Metallica's fastest song to date and simultaneously the most lyrically ridiculous. Let's get lines such as "Bang your head against the stage like you never did before / Make it ring, make it bleed, make it really sore" out of the way, shall we? Then we can address the blisteringly fast riff (a simple scrub of E in sixteenths), Lars' surprisingly deft snare pattern and the heartstopping moments where it all stops and James barks "Whiplash!" Even at this early stage Metallica are wise enough in the ways of metal songwriting to slow down for a lengthy central instrumental section on which Kirk can work out. Too much shredding on top of a superfast riff makes for difficult listening – a fact that the young band had already taken on board.

Phantom Lord ★ ★

The closest that Kill 'Em All comes to filler, the devil-by-numbers Phantom Lord is a simple derivative song taken straight from the drawer marked Judas Priest. There's some enjoyably raw feedback and pick-scrapes as James' central riff comes in, and then the band head down the road together in a moderately exciting mid-tempo rush until some expert soloing by Kirk, who shines on this album.

No Remorse ★ ★ ★

A long and somewhat gruelling workout on a rather boring riff, No Remorse doesn't really get going until a sudden surge of speed in its last minute. When this happens, it's like getting a bucket of cold water in the face: Cliff, James and Lars knuckle down with awe-inspiring accuracy to a pure thrash riff that seems primitive by later standards – but refreshing to those who looked back on it a decade later.

Before this, No Remorse suffers from the same 'long, repetitive and boring' syndrome that plagues the work of so many musicians new to their craft: it's almost as if the band were so happy to be able to play at all that they didn't try to write with live audiences in mind.

Seek & Destroy ★ ★ ★

The first Metallica 'call-and-response' anthem, Seek And Destroy is the most raw-sounding song on KEA, with its slightly wonky opening riff almost painful on the ear. But there's no arguing with the chorus, which practically demands audience participation, or the back half of the song, where the tempo changes dramatically after a drum break and Kirk pulls off a stunning solo punctuated by stop-start introductory passages. Listen out for the upper-register fills that Cliff throws in at the end of each of these.

Metal Militia ★ ★

Not the most inspiring end to this mostly excellent album, Metal Militia is an extended and slightly weak riff on the idea of Metallica as a marching army, complete with tramping feet and bullet ricochet at its fade-out. The song as a whole is unremarkable, feeling as if it had been added to make up the overall length of the album. However, perhaps Kill 'Em All benefits by finishing on a medium-quality song rather than on a speedy thrash workout. The album as a whole is an intense experience, and Metal Militia allows it to finish with an exhalation of breath rather than a foot-to-the-floor gasp. Either way, the song isn't among Metallica's best by any means.

Conclusion

Kill 'Em All is a triumph, and certainly sounded nothing like anything else at the time. Despite its feeble, showoff lyrics – the inevitable result of its songwriters' tender years – the riffs are powerful, the performance is stellar and the production surprisingly good considering its budget and the hands-off nature of producer Paul Curcio.

Overall rating: ★ ★ ★ ★

WHIPLASH
(Single, 1984)

Tracklisting: Jump In The Fire / Whiplash (Special Neckbrace Remix) / Seek And Destroy (Live) / Phantom Lord (Live)

Hardly the obvious choice of single from Kill 'Em All (Jump In The Fire was also selected for release based on its crowd-friendly catchiness and oh-so-scary Satanic angle), the most notable aspect of the Whiplash 12" was its barefaced cheek at labelling the cut a remix (the differences were minimal) and the two B-side tracks 'live' (they were in-studio recordings with added crowd noise).

Overall rating: ★ ★ ★

JUMP IN THE FIRE
(EP, UK and Europe only, February 1984)

Tracklisting: Jump In The Fire / Seek And Destroy (Live) / Phantom Lord (Live)

A simple album cut and the two fake live tracks mentioned above, Jump In The Fire came on 12" – as did all Western Metallica singles – and was solely memorable for the ridiculously over-the-top demonic cover image.

Overall rating: ★ ★ ★

RIDE THE LIGHTNING
(Album, 11 August 1984)

Tracklisting: Fight Fire With Fire / Ride The Lightning / For Whom The Bell Tolls / Fade To Black / Trapped Under Ice / Escape / Creeping Death / The Call Of Ktulu

Fight Fire With Fire ★ ★ ★ ★ ★
Metallica fans who had loved the raw scrape of Kill 'Em All were left speechless by the massive leap in songwriting and production quality and the colossal increase in speed and aggression of Ride The Lightning. Its opening track, Fight Fire With Fire, gave old-school fans a lifetime fix: two decades later it remains the fastest song Metallica have ever recorded, in terms of sheer picking speed. And it has an acoustic introduction, too!

Fight Fire With Fire is also highly apocalyptic: James had refined his vocals and his lyrics to a brutal, almost proto-death metal bark that spoke of annihilation and destruction in the midst of nuclear holocaust. The divebombing guitars and massive explosion at its end should have been ridiculous: instead, they're deadly convincing. Genius.

Ride The Lightning ★ ★ ★ ★
As the explosion wanes, a simple, wailing riff comes in punctuated by Cliff and Lars. This devolves into a mid-tempo riff which is more melodic than anything Metallica had

recorded to date; the band then stretch out into an unhurried. almost symphonic suite of riff sections, over many of which Kirk unravels a series of expertly crafted solos. Listen out for the multilayered rainfall of notes at 3'55", over James' tremolo-picked riff. "I don't want to die!" sings James – yes, sings – as the tale of the man awaiting execution on the electric chair unfolds. It's grim stuff, counterbalanced by the unforgettable melodies in the background. At almost seven minutes long, the album's title track is an eye-opening sign of just how far Metallica had come in two short years.

For Whom The Bell Tolls ★ ★ ★ ★

Another classic from the Metallica early days, For Whom The Bell Tolls (misprinted as For Whom The Bells Toll on some pressings) is a slow, superheavy jaunt that doesn't outstay its welcome, simply leaving its mark with some unforgettable motifs. The deep, slow bells that open the track, the massive crunch of the opening riff; Cliff's distorted, wah-laden introductory solo – a solo by a bassist on a thrash album? Unprecedented! – and the delayed, tense ending, all suspenseful unfinished riffing and Kirk's apocalyptic solo spirals. Notice how much Metallica were playing with the 'thrash' tag on this album. With more than a few light-speed songs balancing out the much slower, more contemplative mid-section of RTL, no-one could truthfully accuse Metallica of abandoning their roots. However, some did just this anyway – perhaps alarmed by the next song, Ride The Lightning's biggest surprise...

Fade To Black ★ ★ ★

Yes, a ballad... kickstarting a long tradition of acoustic departures for Metallica, Fade To Black was the first attempt that Hetfield, Ulrich et al. had made to date to eschew the crushing riffage and speak softly. The result was surprisingly good, a dark, dark tale of suicide and depression overlaying an acoustic workout that never gets maudlin or syrupy. Foreshadowing the grunge movement by several years, Fade To Black pioneers a quiet/loud/quiet/loud structure before strolling off at its back end into a medium-heavy riff marathon. For the first time, Metallica encountered accusations of selling out with this song. Not for the last time, either. But all that is nonsense: Fade To Black is the sound of the young band flexing their songwriting muscles, that's all.

Trapped Under Ice ★ ★ ★

As if to reassure insecure headbangers that they still had balls, Metallica followed up Fade To Black with the blistering Trapped Under Ice, a warp-speed shoutalong thing that showcases Lars' drumming – not as weak as his naysayers made out, right? – and a chorus that nods slightly towards the commercial anthems of the LA scene. Kirk's superlative wah-enhanced soloing remind us that we're now dealing with a supremely talented band, even if parts of this song feel at times like melodic thrash by numbers. In comparison to Kill 'Em All, Ride The Lightning enjoyed a soft, smooth production sound courtesy of engineer/producer Flemming Rasmussen. While it works for most songs, for a high-velocity workout like Trapped Under Ice the overall result can be inoffensive rather than gripping.

Escape ★ ★

With Escape, Metallica – inadvertently or otherwise – came the closest they had yet come to the commercial singalongametal of Def Leppard (their Q-Prime co-managees) or, deadly as it may sound, Bon Jovi. Not that the song approaches the soft, gloopy sound of either band or indeed the cheesy lyrical approach of mainstream metal: but the slightly self-conscious 'rebellion' behind lyrics such as "Out for my own, out to be free" sounds forced. Perhaps it's the warm, almost passive melodies of the riffs, that venture out of metal territory and into the rock zone?

Whatever the truth, Escape is too slick for most Metallica fans and is usually skipped.

Creeping Death ★ ★ ★ ★

Luckily, Metallica bounced right back with the stunning Creeping Death, a tale of righteous Biblical rage and devastation straight out of the Book of Revelations. Pre-dating the later work of Egyptology-obsessed death metallers Nile by over a decade, Creeping Death employs religious symbology – such as the angel of death passing by the door painted in blood – to set up a satisfyingly spooky horror-movie tone that is vintage extreme metal.

Not that the central riff is particularly extreme: Creeping Death feels more like Iron Maiden with a crystal-clear guitar tone than the Metallica style we've come to expect. The undoubted high point of the song is Kirk's awe-inspiring solo, always described by him as one of his favourites to play and demonstrating his grasp of complex fretboard tapping as well as his undeniably European influences. The beginning and end employ the same huge, stuttered riff, with the song's final few seconds a crashing melée of riffage and feedback.

The Call Of Ktulu ★ ★ ★

Winding up this powerful album with an instrumental was probably a good idea after the frazzled listener completes the pummeling Creeping Death, and indeed The Call Of Ktulu (misprinted as – oh joy – The Cat Of Ktulu on some pressings!) begins with a deftly plucked acoustic guitar. However, once it's up and running it's a beast of no small magnitude, harking once more to epic Iron Maiden compositions such as Phantom Of The Opera – and interestingly, the focus is on the heavy riffs rather than Kirk's solos, which would normally be expected to dominate any Metallica instrumental song.

Conclusion

Ride The Lightning is another Metallica classic, with the production budget they finally deserved and an early peak in their songwriting. More ambitious and mature than anything on Kill 'Em All, RTL deserves its place in any metalhead's collection, not just in those belonging to Metallica fans. It has some weak tracks, for sure, but as a whole it's unmissable.

Overall rating: ★ ★ ★ ★

CREEPING DEATH
(EP, November 1984)

Tracklisting: Creeping Death / Am I Evil? / Blitzkrieg

Later reissued with the Jump In The Fire tracks on the B-side, this EP was a real milestone for Metallica. Creeping Death was a fantastic four minutes of metal (see Ride The Lightning), but the B-side tracks were just as important to Metallica's career. Am I Evil?, by Lars' all-time heroes Diamond Head, is a long and exciting buildup to an incredible solo from Kirk, cloned exactly from Brian Tatler's original. Blitzkrieg, by the NWOBHM band of the same name, is much tauter and tighter – a mighty piece of sub-speed metal. The production may be a little kind to both songs (Cliff's bass is pleasant rather than stomach-churning) but the songs have gone down as live staples in Metallica's set and revived the careers of the authoring bands on more than one occasion.

Overall rating: ★ ★ ★ ★

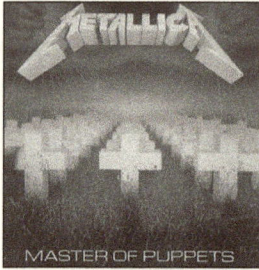

MASTER OF PUPPETS
(Album, 15 March 1986)

Tracklisting: Battery / Master Of Puppets / The Thing That Should Not Be / Welcome Home (Sanitarium) / Disposable Heroes / Leper Messiah / Orion / Damage, Inc.

Battery ★ ★ ★ ★ ★

From the off, it's profoundly clear that Metallica have stepped up their game. Battery is a stroke of genius, from the multilayed acoustic intro (yes, another one) via the huge, huge wall of sound that echoes it all the way into James' clever, twisty lead riff. As a spotty 16 year old, the opening few moments of Battery were responsible for opening up the whole world of metal to me; I've never forgotten the rush I felt as the song enveloped my whole universe.

When James' vocals come in, he's using a refined version of the style he had honed for Ride The Lightning – a perfect blend of aggression and tunefulness, although it later emerged that he was always lacking in confidence about his singing skills. Further high points include the no-brain meat-and-potatoes riff that anchors the song's midsection and ending, this time made gripping by the clarity of the production and Hetfield's awe-inspiring picking precision.

Master Of Puppets ★ ★ ★ ★ ★

The partner of Battery in many ways – sound, riff speed, placement on the album – Puppets' title track is a relatively long, multi-sectioned composition of great acuity and ambition. Ostensibly an allegory of control and corruption, the song's occasional cocaine reference ("Chop your breakfast on a mirror") made it clear that, for the first time, James – still the primary lyricist at this stage – was interested in commenting on more serious topics than the obvious large subjects such as nuclear warfare. Although the main riff that anchors the song – a jerky, unforgettable sequence in E rising to F# — is a masterstroke, sentimentalists will prefer the song's central, clean section, which features James' delay-loaded arpeggio and a dual-harmony solo from Kirk before resolving into the faster, more aggressive pattern of before. The song ends in a howl of demonic laughter, presumably the cruel 'masters' of the title. Sounds cheesy? It's anything but.

The Thing That Should Not Be ★ ★ ★ ★

The heaviest song in terms of sheer riff weight that Metallica have ever written apart from 1991's Sad But True, The Thing… is a vast, lumpen elegy to Lovecraftian undersea monsters that is as crushingly weighty as its subject. The band clearly know a thing or two about how to make a song heavy: the tempo drops perceptibly from time to time as the riff drags its feet – a perfect accompaniment to the most doom-laden song Metallica had yet attempted.

Kirk pulls off an astonishing solo in this song, helped – he explained at the time – by the application of candlewax to the strings of his guitar. No shortage of ideas here, then…

Welcome Home (Sanitarium) ★ ★ ★ ★

Akin to The Thing That Should Not Be in its slow tempo and malevolent atmosphere, Welcome Home… addresses another social problem, mental illness, depicting the inner tension of a suicidal inmate in an institution. "Got some death to do… kill is such a friendly word" muses James as the song, initially a clean-picked semi-ballad like Fade To Black, spirals upwards in urgency and heaviness. When the gear change comes, it's a simple, fast – but not thrash – sequence of downstrokes which build to a suitably epic solo section. Kirk layers track upon track of harmony solos on top of James' droning, guttural riff pattern, ultimately landing on an ending that is equal parts feedback and landscape-wide guitar stabs. Marvellous.

Disposable Heroes ★ ★ ★ ★

Pure thrash metal isn't pure unless there's a fast one-two snare/kick drum pattern behind the riffs, and where Metallica have held back on Puppets until now, on Disposable Heroes they let loose with unrestrained ferocity. A war symphony in which Hetfield intones with evil glee "Back to the front!" in each chorus, the song is a tale of a young soldier, broken by his masters (the theme of control and exploitation looming again) and near death in the trenches. Perhaps, with a song as violent as this, the only possible lyrical theme could be death and hatred... As James' oft-used E/G/F# progression advances (the same chord sequence also showed up in Eye Of The Beholder on the next LP), the song gets harder and harsher, with the only let-up a fantastic solo from Hammett. Blistering stuff.

Leper Messiah ★ ★ ★

Wisely, Metallica don't play the speed card again immediately after Disposable Heroes, preferring to showcase the decidedly weird Leper Messiah instead. Counting in an unusual time signature, the band crash into a slow, skewed song with an eerie, slightly sick atmosphere. "Infection is the game" and "Stinking drunk with power" gloats Hetfield on the subject of TV evangelists whose inner corruption is invisible to the hordes that feed them. Again, there's a tempo change halfway through, to allow a solo to float more freely: but of all the songs on this experimental, powerful record, this one is definitely the strangest.

Orion ★ ★ ★ ★

The song that would, tragically, be Cliff's finest hour, Orion is an almost orchestral instrumental that veers from Call Of Ktulu-like riffage to the lightest possible melodies and back again. It begins with another snatch of Burton-esque invention

162

– a layered bass and drum part that expands vertically. Cliff's stacked chords and the effects he places on them – probably chorus and flange – build towards Hetfield's masterful riff grind and the song appears to take on an orthodox form.

However, after a couple of minutes the sound decays and another bass solo comes in, this time a classical, plucked figure that is mixed subtly into the background. Delayed harmonics waft over the top and then a soaring harmony solo is dropped in from Kirk. It's a bluesy, very laid-back exercise in restraint and complete harmonic awareness: the other players learned a lot from Cliff at this point about classical theory and how it could be applied to metal songwriting. A third bass solo follows Kirk's own workout, and the song dies away in a haze of beauty.

Damage, Inc. ★ ★ ★ ★

It's time for another blast of furious extremity, and Damage, Inc. is another contender for the most aggressive Metallica song ever. Kicking off with another experimental Burton intro – this time a sequence of distorted bass chords, shaped with a wah pedal and then reversed – the song is an enraged blast of hatred towards unspecified targets, couched in Hetfield's spat-out lyrics and supported by a very, very fast riff. "Fuck it all, and fucking no regrets!" barked James as the album screamed to a close, with all the classic metal tricks in place – a shout of "Go!" before the solo begins, a melodic tapped section, guitar breakdowns aplenty. It's a nerve-shredding end to an album – and what an album.

Conclusion

With Master Of Puppets, Metallica finally came into their own. Puppets is the only real five-star album in their catalogue, although Ride The Lightning came close and you could compile several essential collections cherry-picked from the 1980s material if you chose. Without a bad song on it, MOP

163

stands tall as most thrashers' No. 1 genre album, challenged only by Slayer's equally heroic Reign In Blood, released a few months later.

Overall rating: ★ ★ ★ ★ ★

THE $5.98 EP:
GARAGE DAYS RE-REVISITED
(EP, 22 August 1987)

Tracklisting: Helpless / The Small Hours / The Wait / Crash Course In Brain Surgery / Last Caress / Green Hell

Helpless ★ ★ ★ ★
Continuing the classic NWOBHM covers idea that had first surfaced on the Creeping Death EP back in 1984, Metallica released this landmark EP in summer '87, their first recording to showcase the remarkable skills of new boy Jason Newsted. The opener, by Diamond Head, is a blast from start to finish, with the warp-speed riffing behind the word "Helpless!" itself a marvel. Jason is allowed a punching solo spot and the band as a whole are tight as a drum (listen out for the staccato break just before Kirk's solo). Like their take on Am I Evil? three years previously, Metallica's version of the song is superior to the original.

The Small Hours ★ ★ ★
A 1983 song by Holocaust, The Small Hours is a masterpiece of tension-building and builds from an eerie, delayed picking intro to a full-blown riffathon of astonishing heaviness. There's a tempo change for the solo to come in on, of course, and it's one of Kirk's best and rawest, thanks to the live (or almost live) environment.

The Wait ★ ★
Omitted from UK pressings to be eligible for chart entry,

Killing Joke's The Wait is the weakest song on the EP and few fans treasure it. However, it's interesting as the first punk (or semi-punk) band song Metallica covered – influenced, no doubt, by the late Cliff, whose fascination with UK punk is well documented.

Crash Course In Brain Surgery ★ ★ ★ ★

A brutal heavy metal song from Welsh rockers Budgie, Crash Course… boasts a nimble-fingered intro from Jason (who can be heard quietly fingering the notes in preparation a few seconds before) and a couple of sections of stop-start silence (punctuated by the wails of the band) in place of the original section, a piece of love lyric that Metallica deemed inappropriate. It's a gripping bit of tense melodrama, helped along by the fade-out and fade-in, complete with Lars laughing.

Last Caress/Green Hell ★ ★ ★ ★

One of the first instances of Metallica taking the hardcore punk covers route, this medley of two Misfits songs is short, precise and super-heavy. "I got something to say," roars James, "I raped your mother today…" and while such lyrics may be superficially unpleasant, fans loved the song and – fortunately – didn't take it seriously. Green Hell is a fast blast through two minutes of hardcore, featuring the band zoning out in silence, hitting their instruments hard and precisely.

Conclusion

The Garage Days Re-Revisited EP is an eye-opening piece of vinyl: hardly produced at all, it retains a live, raw feel that suits the post-Puppets incarnation of Metallica down to the ground as well as introducing Jason's fat, slightly overdriven bass sound – a presence which he would shortly lose…

Overall rating: ★ ★ ★ ★

HARVESTER OF SORROW
(Single, 3 September 1988)

Tracklisting: Harvester Of Sorrow / Breadfan / The Prince

The first single from …And Justice For All was Harvester Of Sorrow (see entry in AJFA album). More interesting was Breadfan, a killer 1973 track by Budgie that was amped-up and accelerated to heartstopping effect. Although there was little evidence of Jason's bass playing, the huge, frequency-gobbling rhythm guitar riff makes this a monster. The Prince is another Diamond Head tune and boasts perhaps the niftiest fingerwork that Metallica ever mastered – so much so that more than a few snide journalists wondered at the time if the recording had been deliberately sped up.

Overall rating: ★ ★ ★

… AND JUSTICE FOR ALL
(Album, 17 September 1988)

Tracklisting: Blackened / …And Justice For All / Eye Of The Beholder / One / The Shortest Straw / Harvester Of Sorrow / The Frayed Ends Of Sanity / To Live Is To Die / Dyers Eve

Blackened ★ ★ ★ ★
Like previous album opener Battery in that it has an unusual intro, a complex central riff from Hetfield and a remarkable lead section, Blackened is the first Metallica song to deal with the environment – a popular topic for many thrash metal bands of the day, in particular Nuclear Assault. Notice the lack of bass on this cold, icy song

...And Justice For All ★ ★

A gruelling nine minutes long, the album's title track is based on a weird, slightly amateurish-sounding drum pattern that Lars stumbled across in rehearsal but resolves into a satisfying mid-tempo gruntalong. Although the central section is interesting (and more complex than we're used to from Metallica) and the stop-start/acoustic intro raises a smile, the song ...And Justice For All is too much to take in easily.

Eye Of The Beholder ★ ★

Something akin to filler, Eye Of The Beholder is a relatively slow take on the riff in E that James used on Disposable Heroes two years earlier. Although the slightly reverby, atmospheric sound is suitably dark and enthralling, the song doesn't really go anywhere and can be dismissed.

One ★ ★ ★ ★

A true gem and Metallica's first big radio single thanks to its balladic qualities, One is in hindsight a mid-career classic – combining big, FM-friendly melodies and clean guitar parts with a big fat chorus. By itself that would have been a semi-successful Fade To Black-alike combination, but the addition of a truly blistering end section to the song is what makes it a metal essential. Based on sixteenths – enabling a strobe light to be used in the stage show – it's a powerful show of precision and features one of Kirk's best solos to date.

The Shortest Straw ★ ★

One is followed up by this unimpressive gathering of riffs that fail to make much impression. By this stage, the lack of bass on the album is becoming fatiguing, and only the most adventurous or aggressive songs manage to rise above this handicap.

Harvester Of Sorrow ★ ★

Although Harvester Of Sorrow is a song based on a groovy,

decidedly non-thrash riff that sticks in the ear and doesn't go away, its bizarre, almost funky nature makes it a little difficult to swallow. There's some complex showing-off around the midsection that is worth investing time in, but otherwise the song remains one of many oddities in Metallica's catalogue.

The Frayed Ends Of Sanity ★ ★ ★

Heavier, faster and more exciting than the two songs which precede it. Frayed Ends...'s only fault is that it goes on too long. James would often stop the song halfway through on the Justice tour, explaining that it was just too long and unwieldy to play in its entirety. It's not a bad song by any means, but it does require time and effort to take in properly.

To Live Is To Die ★ ★ ★

Like Orion and The Call Of Ktulu, To Live Is To Die is a lengthy and experimental instrumental that demonstrates the players' skills and their knack with a repetitive riff, as well as including a classical acoustic section that builds to a startling solo. Its only words, contributed by Burton before the coach crash, may or may not be influenced or indeed taken from the cult Thomas Covenant novels by Stephen Donaldson – this has never been confirmed, however.

Dyers Eve ★ ★ ★ ★

AJFA ends with a fantastic piece of hyper-aggressive thrash metal in the form of Dyers Eve, the first on-record attack by James on the Christian Scientist upbringing he had been forced to endure. "I've outgrown that fucking lullaby!" he spits as the song, a furious, Damage Inc.-like workout, crashes to a close. Lars' warp-speed double kick drums are a high point, even if they're mixed so as to retain almost no bass frequencies.

Conclusion

...And Justice For All represented a crossroads for Metallica.

The songs were much more complex than anything they had attempted before, provoking them into a much simpler, stripped-down approach for the next album. Lars commented in 2005 that he regarded AJFA as a kind of blueprint for the progressive metal movement spearheaded in the new millennium by bands like Meshuggah, Dream Theater, Enslaved and others, who have taken the complicated arrangements to a whole new level.

Overall rating: ★ ★ ★

ONE
(Single, 22 April 1989)

Tracklisting: One / Eye Of The Beholder

One was an obvious single, and was accompanied by Metallica's first professional video. Eye Of The Beholder remains a bread-and-butter chunk of metal rather than a genuinely exciting song.

Overall rating: ★ ★ ★

THE GOOD, THE BAD AND THE LIVE: THE 6 1/2 YEAR ANNIVERSARY COLLECTION
(6-EP box set, 19 May 1990)

Jump in the Fire EP
Tracklisting: Jump in the Fire / Seek And Destroy (Live) / Phantom Lord (Live)

Creeping Death EP
Tracklisting: Creeping Death / Am I Evil? / Blitzkrieg

The $5.98 EP: Garage Days Re-Revisited EP
Tracklisting: Helpless / The Small Hours / The Wait / Crash Course in Brain Surgery / Last Caress/Green Hell

Harvester Of Sorrow (12" single)
Tracklisting: Harvester Of Sorrow / Breadfan / The Prince

One (12" single)
Tracklisting: One / For Whom The Bell Tolls (Live) / Welcome Home (Sanitarium) (Live)

6 1/2 Year Anniversary Live EP
Tracklisting: Breadfan (Live) / Harvester of Sorrow (Live) / One (Live)

Now difficult to find, it isn't really clear why the sarcastically-titled 6 1/2 Year Anniversary Collection box set was released at all. After all, the only new content was the 6 1/2 Year Anniversary Live EP itself, which was merely three live tracks. But record companies will be record companies, and the fanbase in territories where the early EPs might have been difficult to acquire liked it well enough. Nowadays, in the age of filesharing and CD-burning, the idea of certain songs only being available on a piece of vinyl is quaint; but at the time it was what made cult bands cult…

Overall rating: ★ ★ ★

ENTER SANDMAN
(Single, 10 August 1991)

Tracklisting: Enter Sandman / Stone Cold Crazy / Enter Sandman (Demo)

Enter Sandman itself (see Metallica album entry) was an enormous turning-point for Metallica, and the obvious choice of first single. Their cut of Queen's Stone Cold Crazy was cool – but notably the first time a cover by Metallica didn't better the original: while the NWOBHM cover versions that Lars, James et al. had been recording since 1984 had all been spanking new updates on the rather weak originals, Queen's original cut of SCC remains tighter, faster, cleaner and better. The Enter Sandman demo is interesting, but inessential.

Overall rating: ★ ★ ★

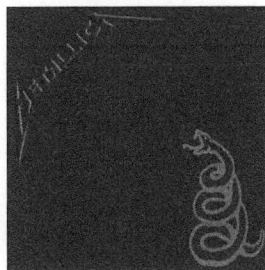

METALLICA
(Album, 24 August 1991)

Tracklisting: Enter Sandman / Sad But True / Holier Than Thou / Unforgiven / Wherever I May Roam / Don't Tread On Me / Through The Never / Nothing Else Matters / Of Wolf And Man / The God That Failed / My Friend Of Misery / Struggle Within

Enter Sandman ★ ★ ★
A genius first single, Enter Sandman – with its ominous, none-more-suspenseful intro, masterful main riff and instantly memorable lyrics – is not only Metallica's best-known tune by metal fans, it's a rock anthem for a generation.

Sad But True ★ ★ ★ ★
Taking the massive sound honed by Bob Rock, James downtuned his guitars for Sad But True and produced a monster of serious power. "Hate… I'm your hate!" he roared, and we couldn't help but agree.

Holier Than Thou ★ ★
Marred by a howling 'thou-ou-ou', this song is just annoying, although it does boast some precise drum/riff interplay. It was mooted as the first single from Metallica, but lost out to Enter Sandman, fortunately.

Unforgiven ★ ★
Metallica shocked a few people with this frankly rather cheesy

ballad, even though Unforgiven retained some dark edges with James' bitter lyrics. This song was the first Metallica tune to employ a loud verse/quiet chorus setup, rather than the other way around.

Wherever I May Roam ★ ★

James in confessional hunter mode, not for the last time: new fans enjoyed this on-the-road anthem, although thrashers were starting to despair of the Black Album by this stage...

Don't Tread On Me ★ ★

Don't Tread On Me is a call to arms and the most jingoistic Metallica composition to date. The riff is massively catchy, too, making it a kind of headbanging anthem for the Bush Sr. generation. Mystified? You will be.

Through The Never ★ ★ ★

As if to announce that they hadn't lost their speedy roots entirely, Metallica include this 'fake thrash' song which includes a dexterous E/B/E riff that many a metal head has failed to shake off. But it still wasn't as heavy as it could have been...

Nothing Else Matters ★ ★ ★

Nothing Else Matters was the final straw for many of Metallica's old fanbase – you could hear it played at weddings all over the Western world as James crooned his love song to his wife. However, many so-called extreme metal fans found themselves singing it after a few listens – it's that catchy. Also, James takes a mighty solo.

Of Wolf And Man ★ ★

Could James really be addressing lycanthropy in Of Wolf And Man? No-one was sure, especially as his hunting proclivities were so well known. But the result was fairly unmemorable in either case.

The God That Failed ★ ★

It seemed that, even post-Dyers Eve, James had much to say about his Christian Science background. This straight attack on the big man in the sky wasn't much to write home about, however.

My Friend Of Misery ★ ★

The Black Album reaches its nadir on My Friend Of Misery and Struggle Within, both of which could have been omitted and no-one would have complained. Could James get any more maudlin?

Struggle Within ★ ★

Yes he could – and so Metallica struggles to a close. A long, slow episode that leaves the album with a whimper rather than a bang, Struggle Within points worryingly to the over-introspective, unfocused approach that would characterise the next couple of albums.

Conclusion

Enter Sandman, Sad But True and Through The Never are decent rock-club songs, and there's an argument to be made in favour of the ballads on Metallica. But the rest of the record, fine as Bob Rock's exhausting production was, doesn't stand up. Not that the world seemed to care: 20 million copies have been sold to date, making criticism practically irrelevant.

Overall rating: ★ ★ ★

THE UNFORGIVEN

(Single, 9 November 1991)

Tracklisting: The Unforgiven / Killing Time / The Unforgiven (Demo)

The Unforgiven may be bland (see Metallica) and its demo

unnecessary, but Killing Time redeems the single slightly with a blast of old-school power from Sweet Savage, all the way from 1981.

Overall rating: ★ ★

NOTHING ELSE MATTERS
(Single, 2 May 1992)

Tracklisting: Nothing Else Matters / Enter Sandman (Live In Moscow) / Harvester Of Sorrow (Live In Moscow) / Nothing Else Matters (Demo)

Metallica expanded their female fanbase by a factor of 10 after Nothing Else Matters, which made many male stalwarts bristle (see Metallica). But it's a hummable ballad nonetheless, bolstered here by two live tracks and – once again – a meaningless demo.

Overall rating: ★ ★ ★

SAD BUT TRUE
(Single, 20 February 1993)

Tracklisting: Sad But True / So What? / Nothing Else Matters (Elevator Version) / Creeping Death (Live)/ Sad But True (Demo)

The standout cut (see Metallica) on an average record, Sad But True is a killer song live. The strings-laden Elevator Version of Nothing… is worth hearing for its sheer nauseating slickness, and there's no arguing with the awe-inspiring Creeping Death, especially live.

Overall rating: ★ ★ ★

LIVE SHIT: BINGE AND PURGE

(3-CD and 2-VHS box set, 11 December 1993, Reissued with DVDs in 2003)

Disc 1 (Live In Mexico City, 1993)
Tracklisting: Enter Sandman / Creeping Death / Harvester Of Sorrow / Welcome Home (Sanitarium) / Sad But True / Of Wolf And Man / The Unforgiven / Justice Medley / Solos

Disc 2 (Live In Mexico City, 1993)
Tracklisting: Through The Never / For Whom The Bell Tolls / Fade To Black / Master Of Puppets / Seek And Destroy / Whiplash

Disc 3 (Live In Mexico City, 1993)
Tracklisting: Nothing Else Matters / Wherever I May Roam / Am I Evil? / Last Caress / One / Battery / The Four Horsemen / Motorbreath / Stone Cold Crazy

VHS/DVD 1 (Live In San Diego, 1992)
Tracklisting: Enter Sandman / Creeping Death / Harvester Of Sorrow / Welcome Home (Sanitarium) / Sad But True / Wherever I May Roam / Through The Never / The Unforgiven / Justice Medley / The Four Horsemen / For Whom The Bell Tolls / Fade To Black / Whiplash / Master Of Puppets / Seek And Destroy / One / Last Caress / Am I Evil? / Battery / Stone Cold Crazy

VHS/DVD 2 (Live In Seattle, 1989)
Tracklisting: Blackened / Fade To Black / Welcome Home (Sanitarium) / Harvester Of Sorrow / The Four Horsemen / The Thing That Should Not Be / Master Of Puppets / Fade To Black / Seek And Destroy / ...And Justice For All / One / Creeping Death / Battery / Last Caress / Am I Evil? / Whiplash / Breadfan

Conclusion

This much live Metallica may seem like overkill, but the much-needed 'souvenir' live album after the band's mammoth post-Black Album tour is carefully assembled, with revealing documentation in the booklet and even some fan paraphernalia. However, its steep price tag attracted some serious criticism.

Overall rating: ★ ★ ★

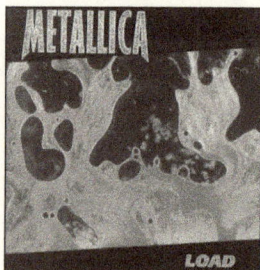

UNTIL IT SLEEPS
(Single, 1 June 1996)

Single 1 tracklisting: Until It Sleeps / 2 x 4 (Live) / Until It Sleeps (Demo)

Single 2 tracklisting: Until It Sleeps / Medley: Ride The Lightning, No Remorse, Hit The Lights, The Four Horsemen, Phantom Lord, Fight Fire With Fire / Until It Sleeps (Herman Melville Mix)

Perhaps Metallica were worried that with Until It Sleeps (see Load) their older fanbase would desert them? Either way, the live medley on single 2 is unmissable. The rest? Gibberish.

Overall rating: ★ ★

LOAD
(Album, 15 June 1996)

Tracklisting: Ain't My Bitch / 2 x 4 / The House Jack Built / Until It Sleeps / King Nothing / Hero Of The Day / Bleeding Me / Cure / Poor Twisted Me / Wasting My Hate / Mama Said / Thorn Within / Ronnie / The Outlaw Torn

Ain't My Bitch ★ ★ ★

Few fans realised what lay ahead as Load opened with Ain't My Bitch, a stamping, mid-tempo rock anthem that boasted some nifty picking and a descending chorus to die for.

2 x 4 ★

A forgettable tune that meanders away without really achieving anything in the way of meaning, 2 x 4 is the first sign that with Load the rot has truly set in.

The House Jack Built ★

The selfsame rot continues as Hetfield appears to be ranting about literally nothing in particular. Meanwhile, the band's riffing ability seems to have been forgotten.

Until It Sleeps ★ ★

Redeeming itself a little with a heavy chorus and a fretless bass intro from Jason that at least implies that Metallica haven't lost the plot entirely, Until It Sleeps was a wasted opportunity for the band to shine.

King Nothing ★ ★

Along with Ain't My Bitch and Hero Of The Day, King Nothing is the best of a very poor bunch: a rather funky riff carries James' guttural chorus atop a reasonably decent rock song, if also worlds away from anything metallic.

Hero Of The Day ★ ★ ★

Metallica do a pop-rock anthem as Hero Of The Day, which was accompanied by a memorable video and wasn't too terrible by Load standards. Metal-heads could enjoy its blistering outro, topped by a sinister guitar drone, while pop-kids could relish the 'uplifting' ascending melodies.

Bleeding Me ★

With Bleeding Me, Load enters its dismal second half, a run of eight songs that are as boring as they are unnecessary. By now, many fans had switched off, and Bleeding Me, a run-through of some tired old riffs, did nothing to change anyone's mind.

Cure ★

One of the weakest songs Metallica have ever written, Cure is a singalong based on a tedious, bluesy riff. They seem by this stage to have run out of ideas entirely.

Poor Twisted Me ★

Poor Twisted Me is just a bunch of empty riffs and spaces leading into a messy, Southern rock-style disaster.

Wasting My Hate ★ ★

Wasting My Hate is upbeat, at least, and appears to have some energy behind it. But this is from the band who wrote Disposable Heroes…

Mama Said ★ ★

Mama Said is a bid for radio and MTV acceptability, although the thought of Metallica producing a country and western song was and remains difficult to swallow.

Thorn Within ★

Thorn Within starts badly and continues with a dull riff based on a pointless shuffle of notes.

Ronnie ★

Ronnie is another tortured-childhood epic and perhaps the worst song Metallica have ever written. Musically, lyrically and in every other way, it is hideous.

The Outlaw Torn ★

The Outlaw Torn lasts an agonising nine minutes and is basically a mid-tempo, unspecific rant: "Outlaw of torn / Outlaw of torn / And I'm torn" says Hetfield, meaninglessly.

Conclusion

An enormous let-down, Load was a spectacular fall from grace despite its few moderately listenable tunes. Metallica had tried to walk the alternative-rock path and failed miserably, with only the abysmal Reload a less enjoyable experience.

Overall rating: ★ ★

HERO OF THE DAY
(Single, 28 September 1996)

Single 1 tracklisting: Hero Of The Day / Overkill / Damage Case / Hero Of The Day (Outta B-Sides Mix)

Single 2 tracklisting: Hero Of The Day / Stone Dead Forever / Too Late Too Late

Hero Of The Day is a weak high point on an even weaker album; luckily the knowingly heavy Motörhead covers – performed in MH singer Lemmy's honour at his 50th birthday bash in 1995 – redeem the single.

Overall rating: ★ ★ ★

MAMA SAID
(Single, 7 December 1996)

Single 1 tracklisting: Mama Said / King Nothing / Whiplash (Live) / Mama Said (Edit)

Single 2 tracklisting: Mama Said / So What (Live) / Creeping Death (Live)

A sickly ballad with classic metal and punk tracks tacked on, the Mama Said single is something of an oddity.

Overall rating: ★ ★

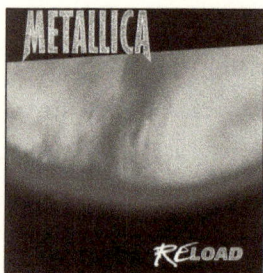

RELOAD

(Album, 29 November 1997)

Tracklisting: Fuel / The Memory Remains / Devil's Dance / The Unforgiven II / Better Than You / Slither / Carpe Diem Baby / Bad Seed / Where The Wild Things Are / Prince Charming / Low Man's Lyric / Attitude / Fixxxer

Fuel ★ ★ ★

Reload's sole standout track, Fuel is a reasonably gripping metal walk-through.

The Memory Remains ★

A dire mix of caterwauling, a nothing riff and Marianne Faithfull's pointless guest vocal, The Memory Remains is easily the worst single Metallica have ever released.

Devil's Dance ★

Devil's Dance is a plodding tale of boredom, with James failing to replicate the child's-nightmare vibe of Enter Sandman.

The Unforgiven II ★ ★

The Unforgiven II opens with an almost old-school metal-style dual lead riff, but basically the soft, cheesy ballad-like structure is nothing new.

Better Than You ★

Better Than You is just terrible, with a dull, repetitive riff that ambles along irritatingly – almost willing the listener's finger to hit the Skip button.

Slither ★

Slither boasts a nauseatingly cheery, upbeat motif and then settles into turgid, overly 'rock' mode.

Carpe Diem Baby ★

Carpe Diem Baby has nothing to recommend it other than a slightly doomy, atmospheric bridge.

Bad Seed ★

Bad Seed is staccato riffing of the dullest order, although it has a great solo from Kirk.

Where The Wild Things Are ★ ★

Where The Wild Things Are is moderately interesting, with some satisfyingly dark chords — but at seven minutes long it inevitably outstays its welcome.

Prince Charming ★

Prince Charming is based on punchy, stop-start riffing and fails on all levels.

Low Man's Lyric ★ ★

Low Man's Lyric is serviceable, with a hurdy-gurdy and violin which is actually pleasant. James' self-consciously 'sensitive' singing lets the song down, though.

Attitude ★

Attitude is like sub-Aerosmith FM rock and utterly depressing.

Fixxxer ★

Fixxxer is another long album filler, with unmemorable riffs and too much wah pedal from Kirk.

Conclusion

Metallica's rapid descent into alt.rock mediocrity seemed complete. How could a band that had been so great fall so far?

Overall rating: ★

THE MEMORY REMAINS
(Single, 22 November 1997)

Single 1 tracklisting: The Memory Remains / Fuel For Fire (work in progress version of Fuel) / The Memory Remains (Demo)

Single 2 tracklisting: The Memory Remains / The Outlaw Torn (Unencumbered Version) / King Nothing (KMFDM Tepid Mix)

While the work-in-progress version of Fuel is interesting, The Memory Remains and its remixes are truly dire.

Overall rating: ★

THE UNFORGIVEN II
(Single, 7 March 1998)

Single 1 tracklisting: The Unforgiven II / Helpless (Live) / The Four Horsemen (Live) / Of Wolf And Man (Live)

Single 2 tracklisting: The Unforgiven II / The Thing That Should Not Be (Live) / The Memory Remains (Live) / King Nothing (Live)

Single 3 tracklisting: The Unforgiven II / No Remorse (Live) / Am I Evil (Live) / The Unforgiven II (Demo)

Multiformatted as a single by Metallica's record label Mercury – clearly in hopes that it would hit big as Reload's commercial ballad – The Unforgiven II isn't a terrible song by any means, but doesn't deserve much attention. The B-sides are merely functional.

Overall rating: ★ ★

FUEL
(Single, 4 July 1998)

Tracklisting: Fuel / Fuel (Live) / Sad But True (Live) / Nothing Else Matters (Live)

A collection of post-thrash Metallica tunes, the Fuel single is worth chasing up if you can stand the maudlin live version of Nothing Else Matters.

Overall rating: ★ ★

GARAGE INC.
(Album, 5 December 1998)

Disc 1 tracklisting: Free Speech For The Dumb / It's Electric / Sabbra Cadabbra / Turn The Page / Die, Die My Darling / Loverman / Mercyful Fate / Astronomy / Whiskey In The Jar / Tuesday's Gone / The More I See

The first covers disc is a mixed bag, with Metallica's version of Discharge's Free Speech For The Dumb and Whiskey In The Jar, plus a medley of Mercyful Fate riffs, worth seeking out. The rest is unremarkable, although the all-star jam on Lynyrd Skynyrd's Tuesday's Gone is interesting.

Overall rating: ★ ★

Disc 2 tracklisting: Helpless / The Small Hours / The Wait / Crash Course In Brain Surgery / Last Caress/Green Hell / Am I Evil? / Blitzkrieg / Breadfan / The Prince / Stone Cold Crazy / So What / Killing Time / Overkill / Damage Case / Stone Dead Forever / Too Late Too Late

A welcome collection of the previous covers that Metallica had recorded to date, disc 2 contains gems such as the otherwise unavailable Garage Days Re-Revisited EP and the early Creeping Death and Jump In The Fire B-sides. The Prince and Breadfan are saddening reminders of how feral Metallica once were.

Overall rating: ★ ★ ★ ★

WHISKEY IN THE JAR
(Single, 27 February 1999)

Single 1 tracklisting: Whiskey In The Jar / Blitzkrieg (Live) / The Prince (Live)

Single 2 tracklisting: Whiskey In The Jar / The Small Hours (Live) / Killing Time (Live)

Single 3 tracklisting: Whiskey In The Jar / Last Caress / Green Hell (Live) / Whiskey in The Jar (Live)

Although its promo CD had been emblazoned with poor reviews of the Garage Inc. collection, Whiskey In The Jar had no real need to be paranoid: it was a decent effort. All the B-sides seemed aimed directly at pleasing old-school fans.

Overall rating: ★ ★ ★

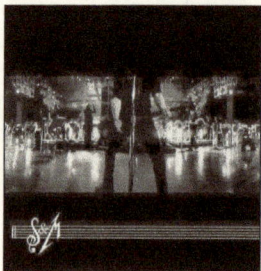

S&M
(Album, 4 December 1999)

Disc 1 tracklisting: The Ecstasy Of Gold / The Call Of Ktulu / Master Of Puppets / Of Wolf And Man / The Thing That Should Not Be / Fuel / The Memory Remains / No Leaf Clover / Hero Of The Day / Devil's Dance / Bleeding Me

Disc 2 tracklisting: Nothing Else Matters / Until It Sleeps /

For Whom The Bell Tolls / Human / Wherever I May Roam / Outlaw Torn / Sad But True / One / Enter Sandman / Battery

Ambitious and beautifully executed, S&M works well in parts but is flat in others. When Michael Kamen's orchestration is restrained, the new versions of Metallica classics work moderately well – The Call Of Ktulu, The Thing That Should Not Be and One in particular. But when the cheese quotient is exceeded – Nothing Else Matters, for instance – the listener wants to gag.

Overall rating: ★ ★ ★

ST. ANGER
(Album, 5 June 2003)

Disc 1 (audio) tracklisting: Frantic / St. Anger / Some Kind Of Monster / Dirty Window / Invisible Kid / My World / Shoot Me Again / Sweet Amber / The Unnamed Feeling / Purify / All Within My Hands

Frantic ★ ★
Frantic has a staccato, immediate intro and fans were divided by Hetfield's barked gasp of "Frantic-tick-tick-tick-tick-tick-tock", but the song is disorganised and sounds terrible.

St. Anger ★ ★
St. Anger does at least have a fully-fledged thrash riff, 14 years since Dyers Eve. But the atonal picking and off-key vocal make it hard going.

Some Kind Of Monster ★
Some Kind Of Monster is eight and a half minutes of doomy, downtuned dullness. Avoid.

Dirty Window ★

Its slightly Led Zeppelin-esque riff, machine-like drum sound, James' shrill wail of 'I' and a high-pitched laugh halfway through make Dirty Window slightly ridiculous.

Invisible Kid ★

Invisible Kid's lyrics could have been knocked up by an eight-year-old. Embarrassing.

My World ★ ★

My World is more rock riffing than genuine metal: a repeated growl of 'It's my world' doesn't constitute a chorus. A more powerful section at the end can't redeem the song.

Shoot Me Again ★ ★

Shoot Me Again is better, but the constant stop-start trick at the end of each verse line becomes a little irksome. Its last section boasts a fast drum pattern.

Sweet Amber ★ ★

Sweet Amber is a partial return to form, with a standard thrash metal intro.

The Unnamed Feeling ★

The Unnamed Feeling is dull, although the mellow chorus, with a simple, droned guitar line, works.

Purify ★ ★

On Purify, Lars and James are fighting with each other for space and Bob Rock's bass part gets in the way. But it's a high point on a low-ranking album.

All Within My Hands ★ ★

All Within My Hands has real rage, with its closing section, starting at 7:27, a malevolent, three-chord riff overlaid with Hetfield's insane screams of 'Kill, kill, kill!"

Disc 2 (DVD) tracklisting: Frantic / St. Anger / Some Kind Of Monster / Dirty Window / Invisible Kid / My World / Shoot Me Again / Sweet Amber / The Unnamed Feeling / Purify / All Within My Hands

The DVD section of St. Anger is much better than the audio version, partly because the sound is mixed so differently and because the live band – even in the rehearsal room at Metallica HQ – can't help but be dynamic viewing. Trujillo is an awe-inspiring sight from start to finish.

Conclusion

Let down by a hideous sound – Lars' snare is just agonising to listen to – and weak songs, St. Anger is a below-average album despite its occasional bursts of inspiration. The much-vaunted anger and rage that was supposedly inside every riff is drowned out by Bob Rock's deliberately amateurish mix, and many fans have written Metallica off completely ever since. Fortunately, they are still a formidable live force: but only time will tell if they can recover from this latest career nadir.

Overall rating: ★ ★

ST. ANGER

(Single, 23 June 2004)

Single 1 tracklisting: St. Anger / Commando / Today Your Love / Tomorrow Your World

Single 2 tracklisting: St. Anger / Now I Wanna Sniff Some Glue / Cretin Hop / St. Anger (Video)

St. Anger the song was bewildering, but the Ramones B-sides were good enough – if you were a punk fan, anyway.

Overall rating: ★ ★

FRANTIC
(Single, 23 September 2004)

Single 1 tracklisting: Frantic / Blackened (Live) / Harvester Of Sorrow (Live) / Frantic (Video)

Single 2 tracklisting: Frantic / No Remorse (Live) / Welcome Home (Sanitarium) (Live)

Despite its promising intro, Frantic left many listeners exactly that – and the old-school single B-sides smacked of desperation.

Overall rating: ★ ★

THE UNNAMED FEELING
(EP, 12 January 2004)

Tracklisting: The Unnamed Feeling / The Four Horsemen (Live In Paris) / Damage, Inc. (Live In Paris) / Leper Messiah (Live In Paris) / Motorbreath (Live In Paris) / Ride The Lightning (Live In Paris) / Hit The Lights (Live In Paris) / The Unnamed Feeling (Video)

Ignore the hideous title track and savour the fabulous live set that follows, with Rob Trujillo's mighty presence driving the band forward.

Overall rating: ★ ★ ★

VIDEOS/DVDs

CLIFF 'EM ALL
(1987)

A must-have memento of the early days, when metal was metal, beer was beer and the greatest metal bassist ever stalked the stages of the earth.

Overall rating: ★ ★ ★ ★

A YEAR AND A HALF IN THE LIFE OF...
(1992)

An excellent two-part insight into the recording of the Black Album, rows with Bob Rock and all, and the ensuing tour. Highly recommended.

Overall rating: ★ ★ ★

CUNNING STUNTS
(1997)

A moderately interesting live show from between Load and Reload. The faked stage disaster is still eye-opening stuff.

Overall rating: ★ ★ ★

S&M
(1999)

The new songs may be weak, but the live spectacle is still worth taking in.

Overall rating: ★ ★ ★

SOME KIND OF MONSTER
(Feature film, 2004)

Unmissable document of Metallica's struggle with Jason's departure, almost a decade of critical derision, internal tensions, jaded-millionaire angst and (in James' case) alcohol addiction. The Berlinger/ Sinofsky directing team delve deep into the sometimes laughable therapy sessions that Metallica endure, as well as the ensuing recruitment of Trujillo and the recording of St. Anger. With commendable honesty, Metallica leave in scenes in which they appear like spoiled rock star brats. The DVD version is the one to have, with several hours of footage that didn't make it into the final cut.

Overall rating: ★ ★ ★ ★

ABOUT CODA BOOKS

Most Coda books are edited and endorsed by Emmy Award winning filmmaker and concert promoter Bob Carruthers. Over the last 20 years Bob has filmed and promoted tours, concerts and made documentaries all over Britain and Europe in venues ranging from Hammersmith Odeon to Murrayfield Stadium, with artists such as Bryan Adams, Spandau Ballet, Jethro Tull, Status Quo and Katherine Jenkins.

The 'Uncensored On the Record' series explores the careers of many of music's greatest legends, encompassing a wide range of genres including classic rock, pop, heavy metal, punk, country, classical and soul.

For more information visit **www.codabooks.com**.

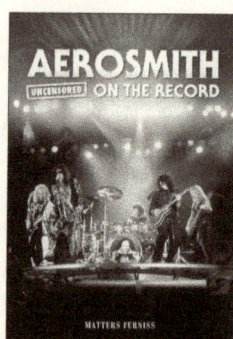

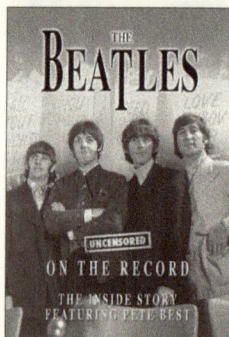

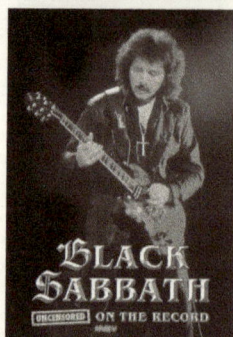

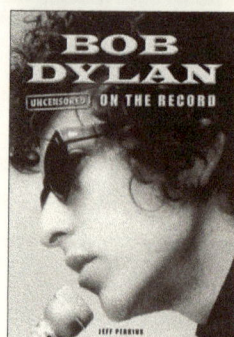

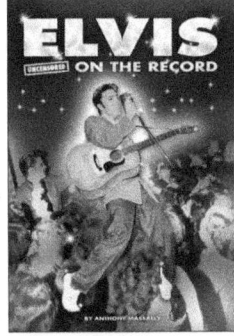

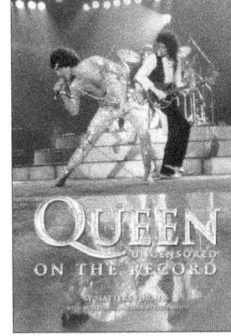

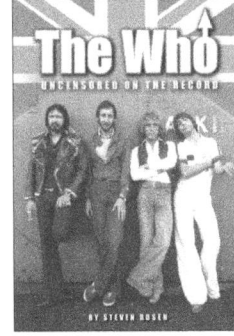